WHERE DID ALL THE GOOD RECRUITERS GO?

TARA LESCOTT

WHERE DID ALL THE GOOD RECRUITERS GO?

SECRET STRATEGIES THAT WILL UNLEASH THE FULL POTENTIAL OF YOUR RECRUITMENT BUSINESS

REVEALED: The secret talent attraction strategies of an award winning Rec2Rec

WITH FOREWORD BY DEEDEE DOKE

WHERE DID ALL THE GOOD RECRUITERS GO?

Secret Strategies TO Unleash The Full Potential Of Your Recruitment Business

© 2018 Tara Lescott

ISBN-13: 9781987633757
ISBN-10: 198763375X

Published in Cambridge, United Kingdom.

CONTENTS

PART TWO

PART THREE

FOREWORD

Ever hear the expression 'The cobbler's children go barefoot'? What it means is, a trade professional may excel at providing services or products to the outside world but neglects his or her own needs.

For Recruiters, this truism, proverb or cliché – your choice! – resonates and reverberates like few others: while building an entire business on one's ability to tap into the right talent for paying customers, Recruiters too often make a mess of it in recruiting and retaining the talent their own business cries out for.

In fairness, it's not only Recruiters who fall prey to the inability to take care of their own professional requirements. Do doctors operate on themselves? Do dentists pull their own teeth out? Hopefully not. They're too close to the situation! And that's how Recruiters relate to their businesses–it's almost a physical part of them–and we all know what that means: hefty portions of clarity, logic and objectivity fly out the window, not to be seen again until they've hired the wrong person and valuable time is being lost figuring out how to effect a no-fault divorce.

Enter the recruitment-to-recruitment specialist.

When I first joined the Recruitment industry, as editor of Recruiter magazine, the notion that some Recruitment firms specialised in Recruiting Recruiters for other Recruitment firms jarred a bit. "Doctor, heal thyself!" was the phrase that came to mind then. However, the realisation eventually dawned that the Recruitment-to-Recruitment, or Rec2Rec, service was needed. Really needed. Virtually every Recruitment Leader I met in those early days told me that finding the right people for his or her own business was without a doubt the most critical challenge they had. An action-packed decade or so later, that's still the biggest bugbear owners, CEOs, MDs wrestle with. Or so they tell me, and I have no reason not to believe (most of) them.

Anyway.

Let me digress a bit by giving you just a soupçon of info about what it's like to be the editor of Recruiter magazine – or as I refer to myself, the Editrix. My job requires the dispensation of a whole lotta tough love. I love Recruitment. I truly believe that there is no more meaningful job in the world, that of matching people up with the right roles in the right organisation. Sometimes even Recruiters themselves don't share my enthusiasm for their mission in life, which makes me sad, but part of my own mission in life is to help Recruiters understand that what they do is valuable and important. And often, it's a very big part of my job to help them understand that Recruiters are different from other people and need different kinds of information than, say, an Accountant or a Retail Clerk about their own careers and businesses.

It's an even bigger part of my job to tell PRs – and tell them and tell them and tell them – that Recruiters are a unique segment of the business world who are worlds away from requiring the basic job seeking information doled out to the mainstream masses of Metro readers who need something to read on their commute. Please!

What is even sadder is the hourly or daily encounter with some hapless marketing executive from a Recruitment consultancy who has no idea what the business he or she works for does, or that 95% of all Recruitment firms tend to promote themselves in the same way. If a Recruitment company hasn't got the insight, the clear-eyed focus and understanding of who it is to effectively promote itself to its own industry, how on Earth can it assert a USP to the right prospective employees, attract them, recruit them, and retain them? You get the picture.

Consider this book a big dose of tough love – this time from the one and only Tara Lescott.

A few years ago a Recruiter's own job site was populated with careers advice that would have been appropriate for entry-level job seekers in just about any profession except Recruitment. This situation demanded change – and quickly. I contacted a few Recruitment industry specialists to see if they could come up with genuinely insightful commentary to offer for Recruiters who were either looking for new jobs or needed a knowledgeable take on the state of hiring in the Recruitment market specifically. Tara responded quickly and with just the sharp, articulate and to-the-point expertise that is her unmistakable calling card.

I'm delighted that Tara continues to deliver brilliant advice and commentary on Recruitment careers to Recruiter – her expertise gained from years at a major corporate Recruitment firm and then pinpointing talent for other Recruiters is a gold mine, benefitting both Recruiter job seekers and Recruitment businesses in need of new talent or talent advice. I also appreciate Tara's direct approach. She speaks her mind, no doubt about it.

And here is her expertise, signed, sealed and delivered to you with directness and warmth. Read and learn. A little firm discipline never hurts.

DeeDee Doke

Editor (or Editrix)

Recruiter/recruiter.co.uk

INTRODUCTION

Without doubt the no.1 challenge, and key to success, for any recruitment business is the acquisition and retention of their own fee generating staff.

I have written this book to help **you**, the recruitment agency leader, to unlock this key critical obstacle to your ultimate success.

We both know that if you can acquire and retain the best people, both you and your business will be successful.

I have spent 20 years of my life in recruitment. And I have learned the hard way how to lead and manage people, despite finding the actual job of recruitment (running a desk) itself relatively easy.

Even at the most successful point in my management career, leading high performing teams within the most profitable region of one of the world's largest recruitment businesses, I still couldn't fully unlock the issue of talent attraction.

It was only in the last seven years, since launching a Rec2Rec and consultancy to the industry that I finally had the time and resources to solve this issue.

It has not been easy (or pretty) and in the early days I had no choice but to rapidly accept that my previous 14 years of recruitment experience was largely useless when it came to successfully recruiting recruiters for recruitment agencies. I can't even begin to describe to you what a complex business that is!

But because I had no choice but to make my business successful, I simply had no option but to figure it out. I was under pressure to develop strategies that actually got the results I needed for my clients, my candidates and the very survival of my business. I was in–'*All in*'–and failure was not an option.

It was frustrating, expensive and testing to get there. But get there I did.

And now I want to share what I have learned with you.

So why would I want to share this with you I hear you ask?

Well my business is safe; the need for great recruiters never seems to diminish (and I launched in the recession). I know I can afford to help you to improve your business, and improve your own direct hiring methods and still continue to build a profitable business myself. There's room for both.

I want to share this because I genuinely want the recruitment industry to thrive. I love recruitment and I think it's struggling as an industry. Our seeming lack of solutions to our persistent challenge, namely the recruitment, training and development of our own staff, is hurting us.

Our inability to make quality hires, at the right volume, is stunting our growth as both individual businesses and as an industry as a whole. It's leading to poor compromises, which in turn leads to poor service to clients and candidates, which in turn hurts us all as inevitably our reputation as a profession is damaged. And that really bothers me.

I'm secure enough to know that clients old and new will still need the help of my Rec2Rec business. Just because I share these direct hiring strategies with you it doesn't automatically follow that most of you won't still need me, or rather my business.

I am certain that my business can remain healthy and continue to grow while you also improve the volume and quality of your own direct hires.

Also, for the recruitment geek that I really am, this is where I get my feel-good factor.

Don't get me wrong, I love helping Recruiters to find their dream role and yes I love helping my clients fill that critical vacancy. But the feeling I get from seeing a business totally transform? The kick I get from going into the trenches with my clients to completely redesign their own bespoke attraction strategies? The satisfaction I get from seeing the impact I have had??? Wow–it's something that's hard to beat and I don't mind admitting that.

I know how brave you have to be to launch and lead your own business in recruitment. I know your struggle, I know the isolation you can feel as you hit a wall that nobody else really understands and I know how transformational it can be to finally attract and retain the right people for your business and finally see it flourish.

That's why I want to help.

So why me? Why are you, a recruitment business leader in your own right, going to take advice from me?

If we haven't already met then mine is a fairly common story and perhaps not that unique. I fell into recruitment. I didn't grow up knowing what I wanted from life in terms of career choices, I just knew I want to be the mistress of my own destiny, to do something that was meaningful and to achieve a lifestyle I couldn't access growing up.

Recruitment allowed me to combine my ambition and commercial drive with my natural love of people and wanting to help in some way.

So I love recruitment because it saved me. Saved me from a dull career. Saved me from a life with far fewer experiences and choices. Saved me from having a job that just simply paid the bills and instead gave me something amazing.

It gave me the life I always wanted and it gave me something I could excel at. For someone who had a lot of changes and upheaval in their early years, it gave me stability, and something long-term to invest in.

It gave me my husband (also a Recruiter... I know... what a cliché!) and as a result my beautiful children.

It gave me a vehicle to be really good at something, so good I could earn a significant level of income while doing something meaningful that impacted people's lives in a positive way.

And on that journey over the past 20 years, I know I have literally changed thousands of people's lives and transformed untold number of businesses.

Just like you do every day.

So my time has come to help you, the recruitment business leader.

To take all of my experience as a Consultant, Manager, Director and business owner, all of the insight into the many recruitment firms I have partnered with and all of the analysis of the many Recruiters I have worked with and put it to good use.

I'm no genius or guru – but when you have worked with the volume of recruitment people and businesses that I have, you'd have to be pretty stupid not to see patterns and trends emerging.

When you have that perspective it can be a lot easier to connect the dots.

I know the pain and frustration of not being able to grow my business and of feeling like a hamster in a wheel with no escape. But I promise you; your business can be what you hoped it would be.

You can scale it. You can acquire and retain great people. You just need a different strategy and that is where I can help.

Don't beat yourself up. Nobody has taught you this. It's never been available; so how would you know? But here's the catch. Once I share these winning strategies with you there's no excuse.

And whether you like it or not, you might just need a little bit of tough love to challenge your existing habits or thinking; but I promise you if it does feel tough at times it is genuinely to help you.

I know you're busy. I know you've got a never-ending to do list and you're pulled in all directions. But that won't change and neither will your business achieve its full potential until you fix the issue of recruiting fee earners.

So please give yourself the gift of some thinking time. I promise you several light bulb moments of real inspiration and enlightenment.

I have broken down this book into three parts.

In **PART 1** we're going to look at why the majority of current talent attraction activities don't work and why.

In **PART 2** I'm going to share the winning theories and tactics you need to use to transform your attraction and conversion strategy.

And in **PART 3** I'm giving you a complete step-by-step breakdown of what you need to do immediately after finishing this book to put this into action.

I'm not a fan of overly complex business books. As a business recruitment leader, I am time poor. I want bite size chunks of easy to implement action points that are proven and on that basis I have tried to produce the book I wish I could have purchased when I needed help.

I can't make you take that next step but I really hope you do; because on the other side of that step is the business you initially visualised for yourself; and ultimately, the results and rewards that will change your life.

Are you ready to unleash the full potential of your business and finally scale up your tribe?

Then let's begin.

PART ONE

CHAPTER 1

WHY IS IT SO HARD TO FIND GOOD RECRUITERS?

This was a question I asked myself repeatedly as a Director at Hays, where I spent 13 years building a career to Group Director level after starting as a Trainee in the late 1990's.

It didn't matter what regions or cities I led, nor did the vertical niches that I focused on make any difference, the number one problem I always faced, **the absolute number one blocker to growth**, was always the attraction and retention of good Recruiters.

It was a problem I found hard to accept because I am someone that wants to be in control of my results and I have always prided myself on my ability to find solutions to problems that other people couldn't (yep that's my chip right there!). I achieved many accolades during my career at Hays but the issue of talent attraction was not a problem I ever fully cracked.

It literally didn't matter how driven I was, how skilled I became or how smartly I structured my business, without good people my business was nothing.

And that fact drove me mad. I hated the fact that the success of my business was effectively in other people's hands, while I could certainly influence it and come up with great ideas, motivate people and coach them...if I couldn't get great people to join my business or keep them long term, my business simply couldn't achieve the goals I needed it to.

While I enjoyed success, achieving Directorship by my 30th Birthday and leading the most profitable region, it was never enough. I knew I could achieve so much more if I just had access to more good people.

This problem never left me throughout my career at Hays, much as I tried I never unlocked the answer while I was there and after a while, like many of you do now, I adopted a lot of myths as facts and eventually stopped challenging them.

I just assumed that experienced Recruiters didn't want to join a PLC where they felt like a cog in a large machine (*and an element of that is true*). I started to believe that good Recruiters were just too hard to find. I totally bought the idea that good Recruiters could rarely adapt to a new way of doing things.

I also convinced myself that our pay scales at the time just didn't match what the independents could offer. And get this; I truly thought our competitors had the power to deliberately sabotage our reputation with candidates. Amazing what happens when you stay in your own bubble for too long isn't it?

I had a whole list of reasons as to why I couldn't and wouldn't find good people and I told myself the reasons so often I believed them and stopped trying to solve the issue.

Sound familiar?

I know how easy it is to create this long list of reasons as to why you can't find good experienced Recruiters.

We're so busy we don't have the thinking space or indeed the time to experiment and as a result we're tolerating poor results and low expectations.

It's holding us back.

And it's dangerous.

Because now anything that doesn't work, those targets that don't get hit, those expansion plans that slow down, that exit plan that stalls – they all have a convenient place to hide. In a file labelled "blame it on the lack of good Recruiters".

So what to do?

Well it starts with embracing the idea that maybe, just maybe, our thinking is wrong.

And if you can work with me on that basis, if you can stop that cynical voice inside your head telling you there is no solution and instead be open-minded, I know I can show how to transform your talent attraction strategy and results.

So, just for the sake of seeking out a solution, can you trust me on this? Can you accept that it's not hard to find good Recruiters and that instead it is simply that the strategy to find good Recruiters needs to change?

I need you to face this head on for the plan I will share with you to work for your business.

I need you to realise that that the statement of "there aren't any good Recruiters out there" has to be untrue.

So go and test it.

You can run a search now on LinkedIn and find thousands of Recruiters. In fact, you can find over 190,000 of them in the UK. And yes, not all of them are superstars, but they're there and they're making money, as all your competitor's P&Ls will show you.

So they're there.

Feels uncomfortable doesn't it? But rest assured there are answers and solutions.

I want to take you through the myths I disproved to myself on my journey to unlocking the answers.

Some are simple and some are painful but it's worth persevering...

By the end of this book you will have a far more robust plan, one that is proven and works, that you can implement into your business, no matter what size or sector focus it has, and have an instant impact.

If you could just hire two additional proven Recruiters to your business and add another £300K/£400K per year onto your P&L would it be worth it to read this book and put the plan I give you into place?

If you mastered that process could you scale it further and train your leaders or future managers to replicate? Of course you could.

Or I guess you could just keep on doing what you have always done and keep getting a suboptimal result.

Which road will you take?

I know what my answer would be.

Are you in?

CHAPTER 2

"THE TRUTH WILL SET YOU FREE", AND WHY I NEVER HAD ICE CREAM AS A CHILD

When I was a young girl growing up in a working-class family in Essex, I believed that when the ever so popular local Antonio Rossi rolled into our street with music blaring from his two-tone ice cream truck, he was simply warning us that he had run out of ice cream.

That's right. I truly believed if the truck played the music there was no ice cream left.

It was a horrifically brilliant lie created by my parents to prevent three children from ruining their snoozy Sunday afternoons by begging for coins or spending whatever limited leftover funds were available.

It worked.

I never even bothered trying to even get an ice cream. In fact, the lie worked so well that I was actually a little smug in my belief that the other kids were wasting their time rushing out onto the street with a fist full of grubby coins.

Until that is, one hot August day, I saw the usual gang of neighbourhood kids come strolling along our street with dripping 99's and Screwballs in hand a matter of seconds after hearing the oh so popular wail of that damn ice cream truck.

I was so happy with my lie until that moment…

And I definitely didn't feel smug any more after that.

In fact, I instantly thought about all the times I had missed out, all the 99's, Screwballs, cider lollies and Oysters (remember those?) that I could have had.

Suddenly I didn't have an advantage and that felt bad.

But I did now have the truth.

If I wanted an ice cream I was going to have to devise a different way to get what I want.

But at least now the elusive 99 or Screwball was a possibility.

• •

What's the link between an ice cream van and recruitment? You're smart; you know it's a simple analogy (although a very real one–it was genuinely one of many from my childhood!) about beliefs.

I know it can be an uncomfortable process initially but you won't be able to make a breakthrough for your business unless you lose some of the beliefs that are limiting your business.

So, what "lies" are you telling yourself about your business?

Whether they're lies you have inherited, limiting beliefs you have been taught or are just weird assumptions you have adopted as truth, we have no choice but to rip off that proverbial plaster.

Because unless we rip away those lies, we cannot uncover the truth.

It will hurt for a moment, but then it's done.

What lies have you inherited or adopted as truth in your business when it comes to developing your team?

Do you believe there just aren't any good people to be found?

Do you believe every other agency or consultancy has a better offering than you?

Do you think other firms are just a more attractive option?

Do you believe you just can't convert people to offer?

Do you believe that it's easier to just hire Trainees?

Whatever they are, you can't stay under this cozy blanket of excuses that you're currently snuggled under.

It might feel comfy under there but it's a barrier between you and the success you can achieve and deserve.

These layers of limiting beliefs can weigh recruitment business leaders down so much that they prohibit positive action and deliver a self-fulfilling prophecy.

Like most owners and leaders I know, you've probably got lots of them that are getting in your way. You have accumulated them over the years and you've said them and heard them for so long that you are no longer challenging them or resisting them.

That concerns me because our industry needs more firms like yours to thrive so I need you to wake up. I can't have you falling asleep at the wheel.

I'm pretty sure, if you think about it, you've probably had Consultants work for you in the past, or may even now, that have limiting beliefs they adopt.

They probably sound something like...

"...there aren't any jobs to fill..."

"...there aren't any good candidates available..."

"...I can't pay them enough–other agencies can pay more..."

"...the competition have all the jobs...those clients won't work with me..."

And I bet you don't tolerate that sort of negative thinking do you? Hmmmmm.

I'm not criticising you here... trust me, I've been there. Half demented in a global PLC, running a large region and constantly battling my no. 1 issue of internal recruitment, usually in disaster recovery mode of batting resignations to stem the flow of talent lost and desperately trying to keep up with operational issues.

The only difference between you and me is that I didn't have time to find the answers then and I do now.

Back then there just wasn't time to test these beliefs. I didn't have time to research or ask questions. And there certainly wasn't anyone I could trust to ask for a valid external opinion.

So I'm sorry if I sound a little bullish here.

I know that sometimes the truth hurts.

But then sometimes a little tough love is needed. But don't worry—when we're done you will have the solution and if you implement all of it you will see the results for yourself.

So trust in the process ahead, and as the famous quote states, "the truth will set you free" (and make you more fees), and then it's ice cream for everyone.

Let's start by breaking the myths that are holding you and your business back from realising its full potential.

CHAPTER 3

MYTHS

myth

noun

1. a traditional story, especially one concerning the early history of a people or explaining a natural or social phenomenon, and typically involving supernatural beings or events.

2. a widely held but false belief or idea.

MYTH # 1

THERE JUST AREN'T ANY GOOD RECRUITERS OUT THERE

··

Let me just stop you there.

I know we just talked about this a little already but let's get this one done first. It's possibly the most important myth of all to bust.

Good Recruiters are out there.

You can run a search on LinkedIn right now and find pretty much all the Recruiters in your sector or location. Go on do it. You can pretty much "find" every single finance recruiter in Southampton, every construction recruiter in Edinburgh and every cyber security recruiter in London.

There is literally no other sector where the target candidate is quite so visible.

You have what appears to be a massive advantage here: particularly if you compare this to how much harder it can be to identify and source the candidates you get paid to find for your clients in say insurance or finance or operations.

KEY FACTS:

- There are over 190,000 recruiters in the UK

- 7.5% Have under a year of experience

- 14% have 1–3 years experience

- 78.5% have 4 years +

- And guess what? Over 53,000 recruiters changed jobs in 2017
  * as of January 2018 from LinkedIn'

So rest assured, the numbers don't lie.

Recruiters are out "there" and they do move to other companies. In fact more than a quarter of them moved roles in the last 12 months and according to our research many more of them would have moved if they could have found the right option. How crazy is that?

How many do you need to make an impact on your business in the next quarter?

If they are out "there", and they do move and you have proof of this then you can move on and focus on the solution.

So what is the solution?

Well clearly if people are out "there" and they do move the solution lies in understanding how to **engage** them, to attract them to your brand, and once you have them engaged how to **convert** them to join your team.

Are we agreed on that as a principle?

Good.

So now, it's just a question of breaking down the "how".

And it starts with how you approach it.

My first light bulb moment –

the one where my mindset changed

By 2004 I was leading a region for Hays in the East of England with several offices across the region. By far Cambridge was my most profitable and successful office but was equally the most challenging location to find good people for.

The cost of living was high, much higher than any other location in my region, but I was restricted to offer the same salaries. We also suffered a shortage of Trainees because lots of bright young Graduates were snapped up by cash rich tech firms and at that time the starting salary wasn't that competitive (although the training was strong) and many Grads were only ever in Cambridge to be educated; they were from all over the world and tended to disperse to international cities after graduation.

And don't even get me started on trying to find experienced Recruiters back then! We tried but it was rarely successful. So, our strategy was largely Trainee / Graduate centric and was focused on the benefits of our training.

So strong was the training in fact that you could almost set your watch to nine months to the day of a new Consultant joining and suddenly the headhunt calls would start with calls to jump ship by competitors who didn't have the training resources we did, They would literally just sit back and wait for us to do all the work and make all the investment and then try and pick them off for a few thousand more on the basic.

I didn't realise it then but I was about to have what I know now was my very first breakthrough. My very first light bulb moment that eventually led to the business I have now.

It was a particularly difficult day towards the end of the year as I remember. I recall leaving a board meeting with a very firm instruction from the board to sort out the headcount we needed to go into the New Year. I had spent the last hour trying to defend why we hadn't managed to find enough good people, why we still had desks to fill and how we couldn't allow this to affect our budget. I came out of that meeting feeling stressed and I'll admit a little put upon. That office generated a huge amount of profit and obviously the board wanted more when there was so clearly more business to be had. But I genuinely thought nobody knew how hard it was to find good people in Cambridge and I was feeling sorry for myself.

I had people available to help me in terms of our internal recruitment team, and because I had a highly profitable business I also had budget for advertising, but even so I was having to lower myself to approaching people directly. Can you believe it?

Nothing. Zilch. Nada.

And then one day, I was working with a Consultant at their desk and found myself countering a Consultant's reasons for not generating new activity against their live vacancies. Now this was a Consultant who traditionally was a strong performer and who happened to run a highly technical permanent desk placing property professionals.

Admittedly it was a tougher desk than some but on the upside candidates were in high demand so pretty much any candidate was placeable.

This Consultant had numerous live roles on and hadn't generated any new interviews that week claiming lack of candidates as the reason. I wouldn't accept it and rolled my sleeves up and worked at their desk with them to make them step back (I did this quite regularly and I can tell you it had a clear Marmite effect–those that wanted to sort their desks out loved it–those that were hiding behind excuses absolutely hated it).

To this day I can remember talking to them and urging them to look at the numbers of people that actually worked in those roles already... Where they worked... How often they moved...

My Consultant had become so sucked into their desk that they couldn't see anything clearly anymore. Despite being an expert on a technical basis they didn't know their facts and their negative thinking was totally overriding common sense.

Clearly the candidates they needed were there. And when you broke down how many people in the overall pool of candidates they had actually communicated with, in a meaningful way, it was pitiful. This Consultant just wasn't being smart in their approach, they were becoming over emotional about a lack of immediate results. In reality it was simply that they just weren't doing enough.

I realised, with quite an uncomfortable jolt, that this was me too when it came to my own internal recruitment.

I might have a fancy title but for my business to thrive I had to see my internal roles and potential new staff as "jobs" and "candidates" on my "desk".

My Team Leaders were my clients, our internal roles were my vacancies and it was up to me to go find the candidates. I realised the biggest impact I could have on my business was to see my staff attraction and retention as my desk to manage again. And to do that, I had to set myself my personal KPI's.

That was my first very powerful light bulb moment that leads directly to the strategies in this book.

And as soon as I changed my mindset, things started to change when it came to attracting new staff members.

MYTH #2

THE QUALITY
ISN'T THERE

Of course it is. You know this. We have already proved that there are far more Recruiters out there than we thought. There are thousands of high-performing agencies in the UK with big billers a plenty. If all experienced Recruiters were under-performers then most agencies would be in financial dire straits.

So, of course the good Recruiters are there. You're simply not getting them in front of you.

So why is this?

What you are seeing, the majority of the time at least, is the lowest hanging fruit of the recruitment tree. You know who I'm talking about… the recruiters that will apply for jobs and send their CV or post their CV online. The ones that will respond immediately to a LinkedIn message, that NEED a new role.

You know the ones. The ones that the majority of the time, have NOTHING TO LOSE.

You're seeing a very small percentage of the market and by nature it's often the lowest quality.

There can of course be the odd exception. The return to work parent, the relocator, the career changer. But, on the whole, good experienced Recruiters are far too wary to openly look for a new role, put their CV online or in any way put their current role at risk.

But that doesn't mean the quality isn't there.

You're just not **converting** the quality people. You're not **engaging** them.

So, it's not that good quality Recruiters are not out there in the wider recruitment community; it's that you have to go to them, not wait for them to come to you.

And more importantly it's how you go to them that is key.

KEY STATS

Most Recruiters that are unhappy haven't even made a conscious decision to "look for a new role" so no wonder they don't respond to a vacancy led approach! Even when they do make a decision to explore new options there are very specific reasons why they hold back from taking action:

1. They worry that their current employer will find out before they are ready to resign

2. They fear a loss of earnings

3. They don't know which firms can offer something better

4. They don't want to fall out with their colleagues

5. They worry about losing their client relationships

6. They think recruitment is the same everywhere so don't understand what they gain by a move

7. They don't have any time to do anything about it

8. They are programmed by their current firm to think they already work for the best or that all other firms are harder to work for

9. They've invested so much in building their desk they don't want to give it up even though they're miserable

10. They have pressures outside of work that mean they need to stay. For now at least

Can you hear the **FEAR** in all of those statements? We surveyed over 3000 recruiters and time after time the same issues came back.

So based on our research, they are all scared of "looking" but here's the crazy part:

- 4% are looking for a new role now

- 8% are open to a move now if it's "right"

- 28% would like to move in the next six months

- 60% won't move in the next 12 months

POTENTIAL CANDIDATE POOL

At first glance these stats don't look good. Only 4% are looking now? Yes only 4%. The same 4% that everyone else is targeting.

But if you step back the picture is better than you think. 28% of the recruitment population would like to move in the next six months and

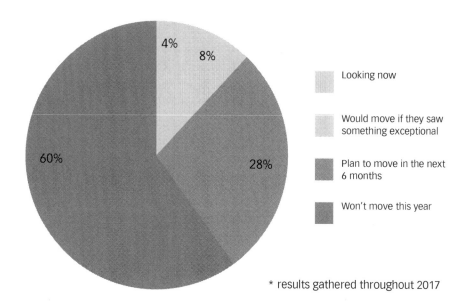

Looking now

Would move if they saw something exceptional

Plan to move in the next 6 months

Won't move this year

* results gathered throughout 2017

8% would move now if they saw something that was **just right**. That's 36% of the recruitment population that you could convert if you had the right strategy.

So really your challenge is to nurture the talent that plans to move within the next six months as well as make your role appealing to the 8% that would move now for the "right thing".

If you can understand what makes a role appealing to them and communicate that effectively and consistently you will attract and convert great people for your team.

But think about it.

A vacancy led approach (the one you have now) won't appeal to the 28% will it?

A boring, standard, same as everything else vacancy won't appeal to the 8% either, will it?

A vacancy led approach will however appeal to the 4% that are actively looking; but then your numbers will be low in terms of conversion and we know the quality is quite often weaker too.

We've got to be grabbing the attention of that 36% and forget the 4%. That means we cannot have an on-off vacancy approach and instead must switch to a longer term nurturing approach.

My second light bulb moment

The one where John lied

A few months into launching Recruiter Republic my plan for world domination was not going well.

I can remember sitting in my office staring at the wall trying to make sense of what was and wasn't working. I was applying everything I had learned over a 14-year career to little effect.

I had jobs a plenty. I literally didn't have to do too much in the way of business development but it was so tough to engage candidates. I had convinced myself before launching my company that candidates really needed a different type of service. They needed advice and a confidential ear. They needed someone to protect their explorations into alternative environments. They needed insight into the types of firms that would genuinely be a better fit for them. They definitely needed me to cheer them on through the interviews process and they would for certain benefit from someone negotiating their package for them.

So why were they resisting me? Why were the ones I attracted so difficult to manage through the process? Why were their actions not matching what they said?

The fact that there was an obvious disconnect became really apparent after my dealings with one particular candidate who I will call John for the purposes of this exercise. And in John's defence he was just the last in a string of candidates that were presenting issues. It was just John that brought me to my senses.

John had called me one day in response to a Linkedin post I had shared talking about an opportunity in London. I had gone through the usual pantomime of him not wanting to tell me who he was exactly or where he worked but wanting to know everything about my client! So we got through the initial wrestling of information to arrive at a bit of rapport and trust. And what it boiled down to was that he wanted a role where the leaders were more ambitious, a place where he could develop and gain more responsibility and where he had a forward route into something more challenging. He had come to loathe his boss to the point that he hated going to work every day.

So all good you might presume?

A recruiter motivated to leave and a proven track record.

Wrong.

His profile was ok but it wasn't that special. He had achieved average billings on a middle of the road desk that he inherited. He only had 18 months in experience. So while I knew I could place him it would have to be with the right firm and with someone that would see his potential.

But into battle I went, completely overriding my gut instinct that something was off. I knew this Recruiter had potential so what the hell. So I drew up a shortlist of potential firms, promoted this guy for days and eventually had 3 strong interviews with good firms that could offer him good desks and targets to move into a team leader role.

I spent hours briefing and preparing John for the interviews ahead.

And on the day of the interviews he texted me 5 minutes before the first interview to say he had a change of heart and his boss was making some changes and therefore he didn't want to waste anyone's time.

Too late mate. Of course you've wasted everyone's time already. But why?

The answer was the he had given me the reasons for moving that he thought I wanted to hear. He wasn't ready to move and I hadn't identified his real motivations. As a result he was never motivated enough to interview—he was flirting with the idea. And he left it and left it until it got too late to reasonably withdraw and copped out by text.

I could get mad. And I did for about 20 minutes.

But I realised this was on me. I know Recruiters. And Recruiters think they know me or more specifically what a Rec2Rec or direct hirer wants to hear. And this is what triggers a chain reaction of completely baffling events and invariably leads to time wasted.

It was on me to accept that I had to find smarter ways to filter candidates into action takers and non-action takers. To uncover the real cause of their frustration and motivation to move and then and only then could I start to represent someone.

So I had clarity on where this goes wrong with Recruiters – all well and good. I just had to figure out how the hell to build a system that worked.

MYTH #3

WHEN I DO HIRE AN EXPERIENCED RECRUITER THEY LEAVE QUICKLY ANYWAY... THEY CAN'T ADAPT

This is a problem many recruitment leaders face; or at least they think they do.

Of course some Recruiters won't work out in a new placement – that's the same for any industry. Some of your agency's placements fail and I bet most of the time you would honestly find that it was a lack of commitment or preparation or care on the part of the employer or candidate rather than your own failings as the introducing agency. The same is true for our own internal hires.

Take a look around you. Look at the Recruiters in your area that have moved company in the last year. You will see evidence that many are there and successful a year on. You will only find a handful that have moved on again in that time. So clearly it is a sweeping statement to say experienced hires don't work out. So where does this belief come from?

It comes from bitter experience that's where.

You see? I can hear what you're thinking!

But the problem here isn't that experienced Recruiters don't adapt. It's either that you haven't exposed the real Recruiter in interview and they shouldn't have been offered in the first place OR that the expectations set in interview aren't met in reality (and by the way that works either way from the employer or employee perspective!).

Let's look at both of those scenarios:

FAILING TO EXPOSE IF SOMEONE IS THE RIGHT FIT

If you haven't exposed the real recruiter in interview then it will be total potluck once they start as to whether they are successful or not. Sometimes you already know this really, even from quite early on in the interview process, but you take a punt anyway as the alternatives are so thin on the ground.

Now if you really want to bury your head in the sand, you might try and find some other reasons for a failed placement. They probably sound like this:

- They're too stuck in their ways and wouldn't adapt
- They didn't want to do new business development
- They just didn't want to do anything proactive
- They didn't get on with the team
- They didn't produce quickly
- They didn't bring accounts / clients with them

But what this really means, and by the way if you want to own the solution you need to own the problem so it is vital to be brutally honest with yourself, is that you didn't get into the detail properly with them in interview. You didn't really expose who they were and take steps to ensure there was enough common ground in terms of values and beliefs or perhaps you glossed over the real challenges of the business because you didn't want to frighten them off.

Either way, the interview was too much of a light touch. A bit like a first date where everyone is on best behaviour. Yet we all know that literally within the first 3 days of joining your team you know whether someone is going to be successful. The signs show themselves early.

So your goal is to ensure your interview strategy exposes the real person in the interview – not within days 1-3 of starting. Because we both know that once you're there, even though you know in your gut that it's probably not quite right, you end up persevering rather than start all over again.

Sound familiar?

UNMET EXPECTATIONS

This issue is linked to the first. As well as getting to know the real person in interview you really must get into what they expect of you and themselves. And you too must be specific about what good looks like to you in terms of work rate, behaviour and results. Many people simply don't get into this until after someone has started. That's like getting married to someone before understanding whether they want kids or not, or whether they want a career or want to go travelling, whether they want to be out with their mates every night or home with you. No matter how much you like someone, you have to be fundamentally in sync with each other.

And you can't just take their word for it if you're establishing the facts by asking simple questions. Recruiters are smarter than that. Instead you need to seek proof of the qualities they claim to have.

You need to:

- Gain proof of their ability to adapt

- Expose their desire and skill for business development and relationship management

- Let them spend time with the team in order assess team fit and observe

- Set expectations with them in terms of short and long-term performance

- Understand what they could or could not bring with them in terms of relationships

- Paint a realistic picture of what you can offer them in the short and long-term

- Be specific about the tools and resources they will have from day one

If you're really honest with yourself as you review any of your previous failed hires then I am sure you will be able to accept that it's never as simple as them not being good.

If you're really honest then the real reason behind it failing was too light a touch in interview to expose whether they are right for your team and the specific challenge you want to hire them for and/or they didn't clearly lay out their expectations and/or neither did you.

It's hard to accept, I know. I've been here myself. We're both human and it's hard to take this on the chin- but if you do accept the problem you can definitely own the solution.

We can solve this. There is a way to do this in interview and avoid more failed hires in the future.

Think of your last hire that didn't work out – if you've had one of course.

Can you see how you might have both had great intentions but simply had different expectations? Or perhaps you can see how one or both of you didn't get into enough detail during interview process to really understand the opportunity properly.

Let's agree, *for now,* that with the right strategy you can expose the real recruiter in interview and if they are right for you they will fit in and adapt.

But no matter what you do, if the expectations set in interview don't match the reality then the placement will fail.

Simple.

Whether the candidate believes you have oversold the role or you believe the candidate has overstated their ability the result is the same.

"THE NO.1 REASON FOR FAILED PLACEMENTS IN RECRUITMENT ISN'T ABOUT ANYTHING ELSE BUT UNMET EXPECTATIONS"

If you interviewed the Recruiter in a more strategic way you wouldn't end up here.

If you had better choice of candidates you wouldn't need to oversell your company and role.

If you knew how to manage an experienced Recruiter in the first few months to ensure both party's expectations were met, the placement would be successful.

Ouch!

I know that last one hurts but I promise you if you think an experienced Recruiter needs less investment in their induction and support than a Trainee in the first few months you are wrong. They need a different strategy to Trainees but a strategy they need because let's face it – a successful experienced hire will make you a lot more profit than a trainee. So aren't they worth your time?

Yet we make this mistake time and time again.

My third light bulb moment –

The one where I had to forget everything I knew.

When I started to build my own team at Recruiter Republic I thought I knew what I was looking for. I even thought I was pretty good at communicating this to prospect candidates too.

I had an advantage over you. I was meeting Recruiters every day and it gave me the chance to convert a few for my own team! Hey–there has to be some advantage to running a Rec2Rec agency!

Anyway, it's 2011 and I am making my first hire. I have interviewed trainees and experienced consultants. I have sold them the dream and the reality of the challenges day to day. I have pushed to understand their motivations and beliefs. And I finally appointed my first team member. Let's call her Amy.

So Amy came with experience of recruitment in London. She had worked in an environment where she had to headhunt every candidate. She had worked in very pressurised and sales focused environments. She was well educated. Most importantly in a smaller business, she was likeable.

So I offered her. I had recruited, coached and managed over 500 people at this point in my career. I was pretty confident I could predict a successful hire.

I was wrong.

I was wrong because what I looked for before when I was at Hays would not work here.

I was wrong because what attracted to people at Hays is not what attracts people to a start-up.

I was wrong because the skills needed are so different I hadn't tested some of the essentials.

I expected her to come in and be an absolute whizz-kid who wanted to be part of something and could do quite a lot of work independently. I expected her to "get it".

She came in expecting to have her hand held and developed over time.

We were both wrong. But it was my fault.

I realised I had to forget everything I knew about recruitment from past employment when it came to recruiting people for my own very unique business. I also had to ignore what I knew about recruiting for clients past and present. I had to stop recruiting to an old template of what a good Recruiter looked like and rebuild one to my own specific and very different needs on a case by case basis. BIG LEARN.

As a result, even today, some seven years in and in my 20th year in recruitment, I no longer work to one profile for a successful hire.

I start with the individual desk and team I want to hire for. I think about those individual challenges and the skills and personality traits I will need to find proof of the competencies I need them to have. I promote the role based on what that individual opportunity offers to my ideal candidate— NOT EVERYONE.

And I use the interview to seek proof that we need is there. Yes I build rapport, yes I promote the opportunity but I always share my expectations in detail and I ask them theirs.

Then we either go all in or not at all.

MYTH #4

RECRUITERS ARE JUST LOOKING FOR BIG BASICS – THEY'RE NOT WORTH IT

Sometimes good Recruiters are worth a higher basic, a more favourable commission scheme and an enhanced benefits package, so if you're not finding the quality you want to see why aren't you placing a higher value on your ideal candidate?

Is it possible that you are trying to recruit for candidates in 2018 but offering 2008 salaries and rewards?

How do you even know if your salary and commission scheme is even relevant anymore?

Because that's what you want to pay? Because that's what you have always paid?

How about paying what that person is actually worth?

What would you advise your own client if they desperately needed people that were in demand but were offering lower than average basics?

I think we both know what the answer would be.

So, if you find a Recruiter, that can bring skill and proven ability to your team, why don't you place a greater value on that?

How has sticking to outdated salary bandings worked for you so far?

If it's working you shouldn't be reading this book.

But you're still here which tells me it's not working for you and I have to be forceful on this point with you. I know your real fear is that if you overpay someone then they won't be motivated to earn commission. But you're letting fear dictate your actions and that never leads to success.

Why scrimp £5K on a basic *(and by the way that's the average salary difference that loses the average agency the candidate they initially wanted)* when the cost of your desk left empty is far greater?

Why keep raising that commission threshold if it totally turns off the candidate that could be billing in your team now?

Why attempt to make a saving here when the cost of constantly churning sub-standard hires is so big?

And by the way the no.1 reason Recruiters move is not for money.

So let's just park that fear shall we?

If you really want to know what leads good Recruiters to take a new role it might actually surprise you. We research this constantly and we run quarterly surveys on this.

TOP REASONS FOR RECRUITERS WANTING TO LEAVE THEIR CURRENT EMPLOYER

1. Poor relationship with their direct line manager

2. Over management of KPI's and targets

3. Their lack of opportunities for progression

4. Clash of values / not fitting in

5. Feeling undervalued

6. Lack of work life balance

7. Lack of leadership

Recruiters absolutely don't leave for the money *(well rarely anyway – there is an occasional Recruiter that realises they are being paid peanuts or just can't survive on an Apprentice wage any longer)* but what they will do before committing time to an interview is qualify whether the role will match or improve their current financial standing. And if, once they start the interview process, they end up receiving multiple offers, then an offer that is much stronger than the others is probably going to influence their decision.

Can we get off this twisted position of "if we're right for them the salary won't be an issue" soapbox?

I hate to break it to you but EVERYONE goes to work to earn MONEY. They work to meet their PERSONAL NEEDS. It's naïve to think salary isn't a big consideration.

I'm not saying you should overpay. And I'm definitely not saying you should get in to a bidding war. But I am definitely, 100% saying that you need to make sure your salaries are meeting the industry standard.

Don't be so stubborn that you incur a large loss of desk income that could have been prevented by a relatively small increase in expected monthly payroll.

Instead, make sure you make your best offer **first** based on what the candidate is worth to **you**.

So yes the final offer will influence their decision.

Every candidate expects their remuneration to improve by making a move otherwise why would they take the risk? Would you?

Take it from someone who also used to suffer the same delusion, you're obsessing over the wrong point if you think Recruiters are just looking to jack up their base salary. Of course everyone wants more. The cost of living is getting higher and higher. If they can achieve it then they'll take it but it's rarely why they seek a move in the first place.

So lose your rigid thinking around this; both as to why a new hire should be motivated to leave and why you should loosen strict salary bandings that may no longer be relevant.

If you don't it's going to keep hurting your business.

LET'S PUT THIS IN PERSPECTIVE.

The average (and conservative) direct cost of an unmanned desk is a loss of £12,000 in net fee income per month (if you take the industry standard of a productive established desk).

But of course, as you already know, the actual costs of losing a staff member is far greater.

It's lost revenue for time the desk is unmanaged + cost of recruitment + first 3 months minimum of non-productivity while new Consultant adjusts.

On average this is a whopping £80,000 plus! You know your figures on this as a company (I hope), so don't take my word for it and don't just work to an average – these are offered simply to show you how to calculate.

Lost revenue is the average monthly net fee income you normally generate as a business per Consultant or the average previous desk productivity – multiply this by however many months the desk is unmanned. Average is 3 months = 3 X 12K = £36K

Cost of recruitment is the advertising or Rec2Rec fees etc. that you spend to find a new hire – average is anything between £1500–£8000.

First 3 months desk costs are the costs of running the desk month-to-month (total costs divided by total desks) X 3 (average is 3 X 5K) = £15K. Even though you have now appointed someone it will take 3 months to get into rhythm and build a pipeline. Average is 3 X 12K = £36K

So, the average total cost of losing an averaging billing Consultant is £80,000.

Jot them down here so you know your specific costs:

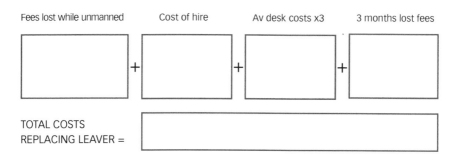

Fees lost while unmanned		Cost of hire		Av desk costs x3		3 months lost fees
	+		+		+	

TOTAL COSTS
REPLACING LEAVER =

Wait what? When someone resigns they take c£80,000 (or insert your figures here) straight out of your business.

THAT'S HUGE. Whatever your number–it's too much.

So now, when you find someone you believe in and like; why let them walk into the arms of a competitor for a difference of £5K in salary that you're squabbling about. That's £5K over the course of a year–not now. We're talking about a few hundred quid per month.

You've got to be more entrepreneurial in your thinking.

Is saving £5K a year on a salary worth it if the desk is left unproductive for 3 months? No.

My fourth light bulb moment

the one where everyone hated me...

I was working with a brilliant Principal Consultant. A £500K biller in HR and to top it all, this candidate had an amazing attitude and personality. I made myself very unpopular placing him, as everyone he met wanted him to join. But pretty much every firm that didn't land him ended up feeling like they lost and hated the idea that I had placed him with a competitor. But it was their fault not mine. Let me tell you why.

We'll call this Superstar Steve. Steve had six years of experience placing senior HR professionals into the Professional and Financial Services markets in London. He was polished and articulate and he had worked all of that time for a well-known corporate firm you would know about. He

---

had built his own desk and was simply made of the right stuff and it was obvious. Working for this corporate firm though meant under average earnings both in terms of salary and too high a commission threshold. As a result, despite billing £500K, he wasn't earning what he could with an independent brand.

Steve was sick of constantly having his desk split to make way for expansion when clearly the only one benefiting was the Director above him who was paid on the team profits and success.

So he wanted to take control and either go somewhere he would gain greater recognition of his talent and lead his own team OR own a vertical that wouldn't keep being split.

Steve had never in his life inherited a single client or contact, despite working for a major recruitment PLC. So he knew he could replicate anywhere he went. And everyone he met could see it too.

Despite the fact that £500K billers rarely come on the market, guess what most of the firms he met did? They looked at his £30K basic, and despite knowing they would have paid up to £50K, sought a short term saving and offered too low.

The company he joined offered him total ownership of a vertical (one they didn't have so it was all value add), a Trainee to develop as his personal Resourcer from day one, and a £55K base. They landed him because they didn't doubt him. They showed him that he was worth breaking a bracket for. And finally he felt valued.

And all the people that lost him were mad at me. Because they would have gone higher. But they didn't tell him and thought I should have persuaded him to join anyway or negotiate.

For someone exceptional they didn't go in to win him. Even though they really wanted him to join their team.

And I realised despite the need, despite how good he might be, blinkered thinking, fear based strategy will always get in some people's way.

Crazy.

MYTH #5

IT'S EASIER JUST TO BRING IN TRAINEES

Is it really?

We all know this is a complete lie but it makes us feel better doesn't it? Because this lie makes us feel we have an avenue available to us that we feel we can control. We can at least put out an advert and meet some people. We can get people in the room and we can make some offers. It feels like something is happening.

But the massive lie here is that it's easier.

Is it hell?!!

You know this really, but you're an action-taker, that's why you're in a leadership role and this is one course of action where you can be proactive and see a result but I warn you this is vanity.

The recruitment process may feel better in that you can see progress being made; and ego wise it definitely feels a lot better to be back in the driving seat and not at the mercy of in demand Recruiters; but from day one it's a total drain on your most precious resource; time. And as a result, money.

The sheer preparation to get set up for a new Trainee, the time it takes to set up their training, desks and logins, the constant demands on your time as you have to break down and explain and repeat simple tasks is nothing less than exhausting and all the while it distracts you and your team from dealing with business as usual and that's before you can even think about adding any value to your business.

Let's set the record straight.

Do you know the average productivity of a Trainee in year 1?
Based on our research it can be as low as a measly £48K and most of that comes in the latter six months. It's true. The industry likes to kid itself that this figure is higher but it's not. Now you may be an exception to the rule, but do you know your numbers on this or are they lost and absorbed into to your wider team numbers? Are you monitoring this? The facts might astonish you.

I am sharing industry averages with you, so feel free to follow this through, then go and research your own specific stats. You might be surprised.

So take the average or use your own numbers and let's carry on.

The desk cost on average in Year 1 is £54,000 *(and again please do your own specific numbers here as this is just an average)* and that's without factoring in the time costs of training, mentoring and management. I shudder to think what that adds up to.

And guess what – the average churn rate on Trainees is c**50%**.

So I want you to do your own company maths here. I have used averages on desk costs based on our research and first year billings which are from all sorts of firms, so make this true to you and fill in this equation. We'll base this on taking on two trainees to demonstrate the impact of a 50% churn rate.

EXAMPLE

Trainee monthly costs   £ 4500 X 2   = £9000

                                  x 12 months   = £108,000 Annual cost for 2 Trainees

This is your annual costs to employ 2 Trainees – a whopping £108,000

First year average productivity of a trainee   £48000 X 2   = £96,000

Average Year 1 Productivity - Average Year Costs

£96,000 - £108,000 = **-£12,000.**

Yep a loss. For spending all that time training and developing two new people! That's without the loss of time and therefore fee income from whoever is training these people and supporting them as they learn.

Now maybe your business has better numbers, but are they significantly better? Are you breaking even? Are you making some profit? Is it enough for the effort that goes in?

Food for thought isn't it?

It gets worse. This example is based on keeping both of your trainees beyond the 12 month marker.

But we know the average churn rate is 50% in year 1.

So if you want to be brutally honest with yourself then you need to take away half of the productivity away as the average churn rate of Trainees is 50% so you will lose one of them by the six month marker and in first six months the average trainee has billed around £20K.

So costs are actually £81,000 (you have to take off the six months costs)

Fees £68,000

Profit £-13,000

Yep to acquire and train two trainees, keep one for the full year and lose one by month 6 means a loss of £13,000 for you. They're average figures. Yours may be different but I guarantee you they won't be pretty and if they are you don't need this book.

So don't take my word for it. You don't have to accept these figures… do your own.

DO YOUR CALCULATION HERE:

Av. desk costs = £   X 2 Trainees = £   X 12 months = £

This is your annual cost of bringing in and training two new Trainee Consultants. This does not take into account the time cost of managing them and the loss of income from time taken away from other profit generating activities.

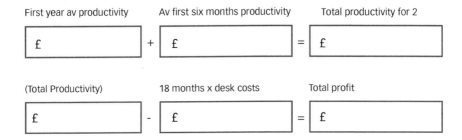

First year av productivity   Av first six months productivity   Total productivity for 2

£   +   £   =   £

(Total Productivity)   18 months x desk costs   Total profit

£   -   £   =   £

Believe me now? It is not EASIER or CHEAPER to hire Trainees.

I'm not saying you shouldn't hire Trainees or that you can't successfully build a recruitment business with Trainees but if you're going to do it, please make sure it is a well thought out strategy and that you know your numbers.

Bringing in Trainees is not easier, it is bloody expensive and it can be quite a slow, long-term strategy. Particularly if you are managing yourself while still billing and running the business.

My personal belief is that Trainees are good when supporting a Senior and best productivity comes from them earning their own desk by proving themselves in a resourcing capacity.

This spreads the load of training, gains immediate value and gives your seniors a bite at management cherry. But that my friends is a whole other book!

If you have a larger business with several experienced Recruiters that are capable of taking on more then sure take on a couple of trainees.

But if you want rapid fee growth the return will be far greater by bringing in an experienced hire–even if they are more of a base cost to begin with.

My Fifth Lightbulb Moment –

the one where I took a resignation at a funeral

I hired an Administrator once. She was lovely. I really liked her. Organised, hard working, funny and diligent.

She organised my filing brilliantly, she whipped the office into shape, she just got it and she was a lot of fun to work with.

But one morning she decided that she had missed her vocation and should have been hired as a Recruitment Consultant.

Now I loved working with this girl. I thought she was great.

As an Administrator.

But she persisted and persisted…and persisted. Until, against my better judgement, I agreed to give her a shot at becoming a Trainee Recruiter.

I reasoned with myself that if she was willing to try this hard she must have some gumption. I figured that as she had spent so long in the office working with fellow Recruiters that she must obviously understand the role.

And let's face it there's a lot to be said for drive and ambition isn't there?

So I took time out to coach her. I allocated some really good clients to her. I took her on meetings, I taught her our process.

I saw it as an investment. I spent 3 solid months doing this and she chalked up a couple of placements by month 3.

And then I went on leave for a close family member's funeral. Which she knew I was attending.

And then called me en route to resign.

She couldn't handle the work. She couldn't handle the extra responsibility.

I was really angry.

With myself!

I knew she wasn't built to be a Recruiter and I went along with her becoming a Trainee anyway.

I had spent and wasted all that time and effort. I would have to recruit for that desk and not only that but also find a new Administrator—more time and cost!

The cost was huge; and the fees delivered were very small by comparison.

It wasn't worth it.

I never recruited a Trainee to go straight on a desk again.

And I certainly never hire anyone without thinking about the cost of my investment.

MYTH #6

RECRUITERS ARE FLAKY

Recruiters arrange a time to talk and then don't follow through,

Recruiters don't respond to messages or calls.

Recruiters cancel interviews or don't show up.

Recruiters come to interviews unprepared.

Recruiters come to interviews but don't make an effort

Recruiters come to interviews and then reveal they just want to be an account manager or go inhouse.

Recruiters get an offer and say they will accept but then flake out just before start date

Sound familiar?

What a depressing set of statements that is!

These are problems for sure and I know a lot of firms, just like yours, that experience the same issues when they try to hire. But I promise you it's not that Recruiters are flaky.

Well maybe some. But genuinely it's not that they're flaky as a rule.

It's that you're targeting the wrong people (probably that 4% that are actively looking) who are looking at too many roles; or your system doesn't identify the flaky types early and eliminate them; which only takes valuable time away from engaging with the good ones; or you're pushing people that aren't ready to take action (the 28% that are open to moving within the next 6 months but aren't quite ready yet and need a little more convincing) and then they cool off and make excuses as to why they won't attend or simply aren't moti-vated enough to make much of an effort..

Let's just let that point sink in for a moment.

Understanding, but more importantly, accepting this point, is the key that will unlock your recruitment strategy.

The problem you are experiencing is a **feeling** of a lack of talent. But in reality the talent is there. The reason for the perception of scarcity is based on who you actually get to meet. But the people you meet are simply a result of your strategy. And right now your strategy is almost entirely vacancy advertising based. And this vacancy led approach appeals only to the smallest and weakest part of the market where you are competing with too many organisations.

Think about it. Your direct efforts are more often than not generating pretty weak candidates, many of which behave flakily in process, and even though you don't rate them as particularly strong, you find yourself fighting even for their attention against competitors.

Sound familiar?

This isn't your fault. Nobody has broken this down for you before or even gathered these facts to share them, so how would you know?

So what do you do?

Well you must focus on the part of the candidate pool that is more likely to generate the quality of candidate you seek and you must have a process in place to remove sub-quality candidates.

Think of your recruitment system like a vacuum cleaner. If you operate one with no filter the machine will initially do its job and pick up everything but will rapidly lose power as it clogs up until eventually it has no choice but to finally breaks down. If instead you decide to keep that filter in and clean it out regularly, it works just fine. It doesn't pick everything up but it picks up what it should and filters out anything harmful.

I know it's a bit of a basic analogy but hey... I think it works here.

I can honestly say I have not had a Recruitment Consultant just not show up for an interview or go to an interview unprepared over the last six years in the world of Rec2Rec. It definitely happened in my 14 years in recruitment prior though and it definitely happened in year one of Rec2Rec before I designed a system to prevent it; so it is possible.

It's not that Recruiters are flaky (on the whole but instead their real motivations are not surfaced and they are swept along in the course of action that they are unprepared for or are not committed to.

If you target the wrong Recruiters (and I'm talking mindset here not experience) they will have a habit of taking action under pressure and then suffering remorse later and bail out on you.

So how do you assess the candidate? How do you judge whether a potential employee is motivated and ready to meet you?

It starts with understanding why they behave the way they do. Quite often they respond to your advert or approach as a knee jerk reaction when they're having a bad day. Maybe a fee split didn't go their way, maybe their colleague got promoted but they didn't, maybe their desk just got split again, maybe they lost another placement or worse, maybe they're under pressure for under-performance and need a back up plan.

Either way, whatever the trigger for their initial interaction with you, they can have a horrible tendency to overstate their position because they think that's what you want to hear and they feel as though they are being "qualified". They rarely share their real reasons for talking to you in the first place but know they need to be taken seriously. They're in pain and want a quick solution.

So they overstate their position. Much like many people do when they go window shopping for cars or houses and fancy a test drive or viewing. Even though they don't have finance in place yet or the deposit they overstate their position in the showroom with the sales person.

They want a look at what you have and they don't want to be qualified out. Right now they want to get closer to what they want but whether they're really able or willing to commit to an actual course of action is unknown.

Because they are in pain they can also become seduced by your reaction to them even though their reasons for exploring new options are possibly quite weak. But they get carried away in the heat of the moment and then regret it later a lot of the time.

That feeling they had that led them to talk to you fades. That "issue" at work calms down. Their pain goes away because it's surface level pain. And so, inevitably, their need to move and explore fades. And they go into denial and wait to the last minute and then send you a text or email flaking out.

They were never going to move. Not yet anyway.

They don't have enough pain. Maybe they do have good reasons but mentally they aren't quite ready to take action. So even though their reasons are solid they're not taking action yet because the pain of staying where they are isn't greater than the pain of moving.

On top of this the people you want to engage are fearful. Fearful that the grass isn't greener. Fearful about confidentiality. Fearful of not knowing where to go and potentially making their situation worse.

Can we talk about the confidentiality issue for a moment? Have you ever received an application or engaged a candidate and openly asked your team about them because of common previous employers? Have you ever asked around about a candidate before you have even met them? Have you ever taken a reference on someone before you even made them an offer?

If the answer is yes you must stop. We live in an industry that thrives on gossip. I know you're trying to leverage this fact to assure yourself of someone's value BUT the damage you are doing is far greater; both to your own company and that of the individual you are trying to do your research on.

You see that kind of activity gets talked about. And it puts people off ever talking to your firm.

So maybe Recruiters aren't flaky. Maybe you're just talking to the wrong ones, with the wrong message and with the wrong assessment technique. And we haven't even looked at your interview experience yet (and I can tell you that many people also need to rework this part of their process too) they're repelling the very people they need because they don't have the right interview strategy in place (more on this later).

Let's look at the real reasons why candidates don't convert for you currently:

1. They never intended to leave in the first place – they're flirting.

2. They're using you to achieve a counter where they are.

3. They're only talking to you because they fear they have a bad career review coming.

4. They want to move and they like what you have to offer – they're just not quite ready.

5. They feel guilty about leaving where they are.

6. They want to leave but your process has frightened them off.

7. Your interview experience was horrible.

8. Your offer wasn't good enough.

9. They get scared that the move will fail.

10. They get seduced at counter / resignation stage.

The list is long isn't it? And I've only picked the top 10!

But the good news is that there is a way to either remove these issues completely or at least manage them in a way that is better for your business.

But it starts with accepting that not all Recruiters are flaky – if they were they wouldn't still be employed would they?

It's your system is flaky. But I have a plan for you… and it works.

"It takes two baby"

So while I would say my business today is a pretty well run machine with a proven process I am happy to admit that was not the case in year one while I was still trying to figure out the crazy idiosyncrasies that came with the world of Rec2Rec.

There was a significant moment in that crazy first year when I learned a lesson that led to a mantra that is adopted and literally quoted and used every day in my business.

Let me tell you about it.

I was working with a candidate that was great. On paper.

Strong billing track record. Had passed our pretty intensive (and newly devised screening system) and had great first round interviews—everyone loved him!

But....

I had to keep chasing him. Chase him for feedback. Chase him to confirm times for 2nd meetings. Chase him to do prep. Chase him, chase him, and chase him.

I got him some amazing offers. Literally got him in with some truly brilliant firms and with hair-raising offers—he was that good (and so was I) at negotiating.

But he didn't accept a single one of them. Even though they delivered exactly what he asked for.

He didn't stay where he was either.

He left recruitment entirely.

And I realised, after reviewing all of the good candidates that hadn't converted, that a pattern existed. Certain behaviours were repeating themselves and were isolated to the candidates that didn't convert.

They didn't put equal effort (to me) into the game of finding their new role.

And so my friends—here's my golden nugget of all time in recruitment.

Drum roll please…It applies to internal recruitment as well as your efforts with clients and candidates because it's not what people say that matters, it's what they do.

If the feeling is mutual the effort will be equal.

This is part of our company manifesto (my team genuinely lives and breathes this belief). If the effort isn't equal we don't represent. I don't care how good a candidate or company they may be, if they're not putting in equal or more effort than we are, when it's their career or business we are trying to help, then something is wrong and we're wasting our time.

MYTH #7

IF THEY'RE DOING WELL THEY WON'T LEAVE WHERE THEY ARE, SO WHAT'S THE POINT?

Good point.

Wrong point.

But I get it.

I hear this one all the time. Especially from business owners looking for Temp Recruiters.

What's funny is that I hear it even more often from business owners looking for Temp Recruiters who used to be Temp Recruiters for someone else and left to set up on their own…

Do you want to tell them, or shall I?

Of course, it can be harder to move people that are doing well as they have more to lose but it doesn't stop them becoming unhappy or feeling unloved or under-resourced.

It doesn't stop them disliking their boss or hating their daily commute or craving more responsibility.

You would consider yourself successful wouldn't you?

Have you never had a time when despite being successful you felt compelled to find something better?

What stopped you moving roles?

Maybe it didn't stop you and that's why you now run your own business. But if you did stop it wasn't because you were successful. The fact that you were doing well didn't mean you were immune to dissatisfaction or frustration. Because we both know that it's often those that are doing well that become the unhappiest.

So perhaps it isn't success that stops Recruiters from moving.

It's fear. Fear of the unknown, fear of lost earnings, and fear that they would make things worse not better. So often, they stay with the devil they know.

And they *tolerate*. Eurgh–what a terrible compromise for someone who is successful.

So people that do well **can** leave and often do **want** to leave their current firm but they need proof of what is out there and in very real terms. And I bet you're not giving them enough information to trade on.

And even if you do get one of these "successful people" through the door what's your strategy?

People don't stay happy because they're doing well. In fact, it's when they're doing well that they often become demotivated. It's when Recruiters feel unloved or under-valued for their efforts that they fall out of love with their employer.

They've literally put blood, sweat and tears into achieving great results only to reach the finishing line and find no prize, no "well done", and no medal.

Or worse; the finish line is not the finish line. Someone just added 5K to their marathon.

Do you see it? So yes, good performers do leave.

You are ignoring the absolute best candidates if you adopt this strange belief that good people don't leave. You want good people, don't you?

Find out what they want to change, lose, or acquire and speak to their PAIN.

Don't block potential candidates before you've even got started.

Do you know the top 5 reasons why big billers actually leave?

1. They feel under performers are tolerated while they are constantly pushed for more.

2. They are not given enough attention or recognition because you're too busy spending time with under-performers who will end up leaving anyway.

3. They feel their loyalty isn't valued.

4. They feel over-managed.

5. Despite all the fees they generate they don't have a say in the business.

"When I lost my biggest biller and we both had egg on our face"

Back in my Hays days I was run ragged.

No seriously. I was never a back office manager. I was always billing even when I wasn't supposed to. I was always out on visits with my team, I was always out there in the mix. I was a working Mum. I was running a large and profitable region. And every month more was demanded of my team because between you and I, I was pretty much banked on to bail out other regions that quite often didn't perform.

Yes we were capable of more but we were certainly becoming victims of our own success. We were the glory team. Highest productivity, best rate of return, best temp numbers, and the strongest perm division. It was a golden time with hindsight. And I had a great team around me; Consultants I had developed into Managers; and we were a tight team.

But it came under real threat in a pretty savage way.

No matter how much I tried to shield the team from the pressures coming down from above (and as we hit the recession this really started to bite) some of it had to be passed on. A firmer grip on P&L analysis was making itself known in board meetings and there became less autonomy.

I had to really push my guys, who to be fair were already pretty much at their limit and had been for some time.

And you must remember – everything we did was largely with Trainees we developed ourselves.

I had no choice but to spend more time with Trainees. I knew I couldn't push my top performers much more so my thinking was that the growth had to come from making underperformers more profitable and fast tracking trainees. All sounds very admirable—yes?

Wrong.

I got so sucked into the exhausting work of directly managing, coaching and leading a batch of trainers and actioning underperformers through an intense performance coaching programme that I stopped giving my top people what they needed. Time with me.

I don't want to sound arrogant. It wasn't about me. It was about them. They needed me (I could have been anyone), to ground them, give them perspective, talk through plans, have a bit of time out away from their desk and team, make them feel good, cheer them on, celebrate their wins.

And I went and cut them off.

I thought they knew what I was doing.

I thought they realised I was doing this for them.

They didn't.

And my biggest biller and one of my best managers, on a bad day, had his head turned by a competitor. A competitor who would ultimately use him, chew him up and spit him out. But on that day and the days that followed, he was made to feel valued. They were giving him the attention I used to. And he fell for it.

It happened right under my nose and I didn't even see it coming.

I lost my top performer for the sake of a few underperformers who wouldn't make it anyway.

And we both lost.

Within a year he was out of recruitment entirely; tail between his legs.

What a waste for all of us.

RECRUITERS DON'T WANT TO DO BUSINESS DEVELOPMENT

Before we smash through this little problem can we just talk about business development please?

What does it really mean to you? And why do you think people don't want to do it?

Could it be that the way you describe it is getting in your way?

Could it be that your prospective new employee's previous firm made an absolute hash of managing BD activities to the point where they now hate it? And by "it" I mean how they are made to feel about business development through the way in which they are managed on it.

It's rarely a lack of ability or desire (although there are some that this applies to). More often than not it's just a lack of investment in proper training or poor management that creates this stressful environment which turns Consultants off.

It's rarely a lack of motivation. Which leads me on to one of my personal bugbears when it comes to recruitment terminology and slang.

Can we stop using the word "hungry"?

Remove it from adverts; take it out of your vocabulary and stopping using it to describe your dream hire.

Hello??? You're forgetting what you know about recruitment again.

There's a difference between what you want and how you frame that for someone else.

Go ahead and fill your boots telling yourself that you need someone that's hungry but please don't use that anywhere other than inside your own head. If you think a decent candidate identifies with the word hungry you're wrong. It sounds negative and desperate.

If what you are really looking for is someone capable of developing and managing relationships with clients and candidates then what you're really looking for is someone that is motivated by the ability to dictate their own level of income, that wants to be the master or mistress of their own destiny, that is results driven. So just say it!!!!! Stop talking about cold calling and being "hungry"- who identifies with that?

Anyway; now I have that rant out of the way, let's talk about the dreaded BD issue.

Let's start with what exactly, EXACTLY, business development means to you in your team. Because honestly, it is very different company to company.

Let's chunk it down.

- Is it about generating their own vacancies? I'm pretty sure that's your goal.

- If that's the case then think about how they would go about doing this?

- What types of activities would they need to carry out on a regular basis?

- What skills or personality traits would they need to deliver?

- What proof do you need to see to feel confident that they are capable?

You see the term business development is used lazily and as too broad a term.

I can tell you now that word means largely negative things to most recruiters and it's not the activity itself they dislike. It's how they are forced to do it, how they are managed on it and how unrealistic expectations are placed on them.

BD can be tough (particularly for Recruiters who haven't been shown a good way to do it) and many would prefer not to do it if they didn't have to but time and time again the real issue is how they are trained and managed on it.

So maybe think about whether you use the term business development or instead talk about relationship management and job generation. Instead talk about the activities the person will be involved with and should naturally enjoy.

You really must not underestimate this issue. This is one of the BIGGEST ways to lose a potential candidate. In your bid to filter out lazy Recruiters you put the good guys off. The good guys that have skill and drive but hate the way they are managed and are simply suffering from clumsy management.

Let's accept that Consultants, on the whole, will always prefer a warm desk to a cold one, don't like heavy-handed management on KPI's but will enjoy developing their relationships with clients.

They are not all working at firms as Account Managers.

If you stay fixed in your thinking on this then you you are missing a trick. If someone currently works as a 360 Recruiter somewhere and is successful then they clearly can do business development; they just don't like how it's managed where they are.

The trick is to use language that talks about what you need them to do without triggering the feelings they are currently fed up with.

There is a way to get what you want, a Consultant capable and willing to do business development, in a way that attracts them rather than repels them.

My story –
the one where I threw my laptop on the floor

So, ok, I was having a bit of a bad day. It was during the time when I was living in Stockholm in 2012 and managing both the business in the UK and a project office in Stockholm too. And as well as this I was juggling a home life that included two children and pretty severe weather (-20) and very little daylight.

And as if defrosting my car inside and out and taking my son to school up a hill via sled (because buggies don't work in thick snow and NOTHING stops in Sweden despite weather) wasn't an aggravating enough start to the day, I was also up to my eyeballs in work across both locations. And like most years around January, everyone wakes up from the December slumber and wants results NOW.

We had so many genuinely good roles on. And our marketing and head-hunting calls weren't quite converting at the rate we would expect.

We were also using a new CRM system and the marketing element of it was a little clunky to say the least.

We had a pretty big retained campaign underway and we desperately need our supporting email marketing to go out on that snowy Monday morning. So let's just say the pressure was on.

Is there anything more frustrating than your IT letting you down????? I don't know about you but the control freak in me becomes savage in such circumstances I can tell you.

Anyway–the upshot was the email, that very pretty html template that finely crafted email, finally went out.

And it went out **wrong**.

It dragged through the completely wrong job advert.

The company information was correct but it dragged through the wrong role.

And I lost it. I mean really lost it. I had the mother of all meltdowns and in sheer frustration I threw my laptop on the floor in disgust (I was on my own I hasten to add–I'm not a total monster).

But guess what?

It was a blessing in disguise. Because the very same people that usually said that they were not looking for a move, some of which we had contacted on a pretty consistent basis with some pretty awesome options, were suddenly interested.

It got people talking to us that wouldn't normally.

And you know why?

When I compared it to all of our other emails and jobs, the only difference was that at no time did we talk about BD. And up until that time we had been stressing the point our clients kept stressing to us in a bid to isolate people that didn't want to make new business calls.

I talked to all of them personally. I asked them for specific reasons as to why they had responded now and not before.

And time and time again I obtained the same reasoning. The role just sounded better than theirs. There was a fundamental shift in perspective. It felt less like what they had and more like what they wanted.

And this was the beginning of the end of our old style of adverts.

And we realised we had to translate what the client needed and connect that to what the ideal candidate needed.

And everything changed. It led to our high converting content copywriting formula–(more of that later).

Our business changed forever–almost overnight.

MYTH #9

EVEN IF I DO OFFER SOMEONE I LIKE THEY WILL JUST ACCEPT A HIGHER OFFER

Damn right.

Well ok...not always... but sometimes that's the right thing for them to do and you're going to have to live with it.

Unless of course your salaries are below standard or you know you're trying to lowball.

Or get this.... you've gone low but would have gone higher but now it's too late. That is the worst scenario by far.

If someone is good and open to moving; chances are more than one person wants them to join their team. I'm sorry but you're just going to have to accept it.

The issue here is not about Recruiters creating bidding wars (although if you keep restricting yourself to the 4% actively working offers this will never go away); instead it's about making them want to accept your offer.

It's about how you make them feel.

Why are you are moaning about lack of talent and then giving people a rough time in interview?

Why are you so keen to convert them but then push them away; and crazier still, expect them to say they want your firm and only yours without you even making an offer yet?

Why don't you want to share feedback until you know theirs?

Because you hate rejection; a fact that can be hard to accept, I know.

You absolutely hate saying you want someone just for them to turn you down.

You hate offering someone just for them to join your competitor.

You're not alone, you know. We all feel this way.

I get it. I really do. I used to do it at Hays. WITH TRAINEES. In some ways entry level candidates need to be challenged more in interview to try and understand how committed they are to the robust and challenging training process ahead in their first 6–12 months; and as we have found out it's a considerable investment to take on a Trainees. But this is the wrong strategy with experienced hires.

Reverse it to see how this challenging style of interview feels.

If a Consultant came to meet you and spent the first 30 minutes quizzing you on your very motives for recruiting because; perhaps it's not just expansion that creates your need maybe you have a staff retention problem... how would you feel?

What if they tested you on your company figures; how would you react?

If a Consultant came and interviewed with you and said they were interested but wanted you to meet other people first and only come back if you would offer them and only them what would you say?

If a candidate refused to give you any feedback until you shared yours what would you do?

What would you say if a candidate refused to come back unless you cancelled any other candidates you already had on interview, as it should be obvious that they were the right choice?

I'm pretty sure I know how you would react to a candidate that interviewed in this way.

Yet if you're like most of other agency leaders you're probably guilty of doing this to some of your candidates. Are you guilty of this? It sounds kind of crazy in reverse don't you think?

I don't know where it comes from but it creates a negative reaction from most Recruiters. It may be that because you have struggled with poor quality candidates in the past and you've seen the damage that can be caused by a bad hire; that you're very cautious, even suspicious, about your candidates.

I also have a sneaky suspicion that this might be how you were interviewed many moons ago as a Trainee. But that was a Trainee strategy. And more importantly that was then...the market is very different now. The whole world has changed over the last few years.

We need a reset. Ponder the following questions to make sure that the interview process is as robust as your client meeting strategy.

If you had to meet a client who had £200K + a year to give you in fees how would you approach that meeting? Would it be confrontational or engaging?

Would you sell to them or make them sell to you?

Would you push them away or pull them in close?

Now don't get me wrong – I know you're smart so you will want to qualify that business, you'll want to make sure you get some controls into the process that you need, but you never take your eye off of the prize and you damn sure make your client feel good while you do it.

Remember these people are not in a functional role as part of a bigger cycle that generates profit like you would get in finance, HR, procurement.

These are fee-generating people.

They're not in a functional role they are in a fee billing role and they have the potential to add serious profits to your business.

They will generate multiple offers and yes salary has a big influence– everyone wants more if they can get it. But I promise you if you build a relationship with them, get to understand them, and get them to buy into the unique qualities of your firm and what life will look like for them in your team, they will join.

If they don't then you have to either accept there was just simply a better firm for them out there or you have to be better at making a strong offer first time around.

Do you know how many firms lose out on a good candidate because they tried to go light on the offer but were always prepared to go a little higher if they needed?

If they needed?

What???

In a market where every experienced Recruiter has in excess of 28 local opportunities in their location and niche?

Offer them what they are worth to you straight away. Get it right first time. That's why others win them and you don't.

And by the way don't just assume you lost someone due to money.

Did you know it's used as the most common excuse for not accepting because the candidate feels too awkward to tell you the truth?

So half the time this isn't even the real reason for rejecting your offer anyway!

You have to make the interview compelling for the right candidate and you have to make your best offer first time.

Anything less is madness. And don't accept *"an offer I couldn't refuse"* as a reason why your preferred candidate didn't accept. Push back and ask what else influenced their decision, say that you're really disappointed you didn't land them and you wouldn't want the same to happen again, that you wish them well but genuinely ask them for feedback. They only need a little pushing back in a non-aggressive way to offer you the real answer.

Especially if you ask them outright for their advice as to how you could improve the interview and offer experience.

Scary I know. But try it. You will be surprised but enlightened by the feedback.

My Story –

and why money can't buy you love

One of my first experienced Consultant hires at Recruiter Republic was a superstar in the making and she didn't even know it.

She actually approached me to help her find a role as she was relocating to Cambridge but I could instantly tell she would be wasted on most of the firms she would have available to her and she definitely wouldn't get the coaching she needed.

I probably spent about 3 hours with her in that first meeting. We hit it off.

I got to know her, on a really personal level. I listened to her frustrations in her previous roles and I shared a lot of personal stories with her to show her she was right to want the things she wanted. That she was capable. That actually I was more than happy to find her options but that I strongly felt the best place for her was on my team.

I showed her, warts and all, what the challenges would be but I also showed her how I could mentor her. I was honest that I thought it would be more challenging for her in the short to medium term but far more lucrative in the long term.

I made her the strongest offer I could based on her value to me and my business and I was honest in telling her that she could achieve more elsewhere initially.

She already had other offers.

And she turned them down to join us.

That superstar is Cheryl—some of you may have been lucky enough to work with her.

Yes I could have tried paying her less as I had to teach her everything from scratch, but I knew she was worth more.

And she knew she could earn more in the short term somewhere else but she had a far more lucrative career ahead of her with us.

Money didn't buy her that day. But maybe if I had lowballed it would have lost her.

Maybe by drawing her in, building her up and showing her the answer to her frustration was far more valuable to her.

Maybe that compelling vision for her future and how that would make her feel is what got her buy in.

MYTH #10

I NEED SOMEONE WITH A £200K BILLING PROFILE

Do you? Do you really?

Why? Where did this number come from?

I know it sounds nice but do you really?

These £200K + billers you think you need can be harder to convince to move, and will definitely be countered heavily. They have more at risk and will probably want more security to move. They probably have some pretty serious restrictive covenants on them too.

Don't get me wrong. If you have a £200K + biller banging on your door by all means let them in. But you're missing out on a lot of great potential candidates if you overly fixate on this.

What if you focused more on proven Consultants, the ones that could be capable of billing £200K over the next 12 months? You're far more likely to acquire someone who is billing £100K + and is proven already but ready to step up.

Think about it.

The difference in salary on a £100K biller and £200K can be significant so there's definitely less risk on the salary investment.

A £100K biller is proven and relatively low risk. They are far more affordable and hopefully you can take them on the journey to £200K. They are also far likely to be moulded into your way of doing things.

Also if a £100K biller grows with you it will create a really compelling internal case study to offer other new potential candidates as you will now have proof of how you can change someone's career and earnings.

And by the way the average £100K biller takes away 33% of their billings in salary and commission.

The average £200K + biller takes away closer to 40% of their billings for the same.

Depending on how your company commission scheme works you might be better off having two £100K billers than one £200K biller.

Do the maths either way so that you know for sure. You might be one of the business leaders that get a shock on the numbers.

EXAMPLE:

Billings	1 x £100K	2 x £100K	1 x £200k
Employee costs	£33,000	£66,000	£80,000
Business net profit	£67,000	£134,000	£120,000

So don't assume anything until you know your numbers. Many of us have "standards" we expect or stick to because we've heard them for so long we don't challenge them anymore.

But is that relevant to the business you have today? Do you know the numbers? If seeking £200K billers is still your strategy then by all means go for it – but make it an informed decision.

Many of us don't have the luxury of time. Time to sit down, look at the detail and reflect and as a result we could be missing a far easier solution.

We believe we have to be busy. And busy usually looks like making calls, meeting clients, filling jobs.

When really, sometimes, taking an hour out to think and absorb the detail can fast track our results.

If your commission scheme means that two £100K billers is more profitable for your business than one £200K biller then another factor that is worthy of your consideration is that two £100K billers will be more likely to grow their fee line more the following year – so two £100K billers today could be cheaper in the year ahead but will also be far more likely to increase your fees to £400K the following year than the £200K biller who won't follow the same growth trajectory.

My story –

about the month I threw away £5K in cold hard cash

So towards the end of my tenure at Hays as an Operations Director I had a complicated bonus structure in place that I won't bore you with here. It was based on several component parts including rate of return (RoR). As a Director at Hays this meant percentage of net fee income converted to profit.

Quite a separate KPI to net fee income and productivity. One I hadn't paid much attention to until it hit me quite hard like a punch to the back of the head.

You see I hadn't paid it that much attention. Because ultimately, even though I was a Director I had very little control or influence over what appeared on my P&L or what central costs were recharged. I had all kinds of costs I couldn't ever get to the bottom of.

I simply had to trust my NFI and productivity to the do the talking and largely it worked. That is until I lost out on a £5K bonus.

Even though I had outperformed all of my peers in productivity, overall fee income, temp margin and perm percentages. Why? Because I had kept more of my staff, I had progressed them, and I had made them highly productive. And guess what?

After finally getting the equivalent of nuclear codes from the president I actually got the figures behind the P&L. And I realised my problem.

I was being penalised for success. Because as a business, my big billers were proportionally making my business less profitable.

Because once they hit their peak in terms of billings their costs continued to increase but not to the same rate as their fee growth.

Most of them had hit a ceiling at £200K–£280K and once there they tended to stay there and to be fair I didn't have a problem with that and who would?

But the increased salaries, the increased benefits packages, the increase NI, the higher-level commission, it all added up.

I rapidly realised I would have been better off with more consultants at a lower fee level – in both cash and % profit terms.

I genuinely couldn't believe it. Maybe you're better with numbers than I was back then. Maybe your salaries and benefits don't rise with time served or your desk cost ratios are different.

But I was gobsmacked back then. And I realised big billers weren't always the tonic for growing businesses.

Maybe I needed better balance.

* * * WARNING * * *

ADOPTING THE FOLLOWING BELIEFS WILL
CAUSE HARM TO YOUR BUSINESS.

IF YOU FIND YOURSELF ADOPTING OR REPEATING
ANY OF THE BELOW PLEASE GO AND BEAT YOUR HEAD
AGAINST THE NEAREST WALL

THE TEN DEADLY BULLSH*T BELIEFS OF
RECRUITMENT AGENCY LEADERS

1. There are no good Recruiters out there

2. The ones that are out there are poor quality

3. An experienced hire would never adapt in my team

4. Recruiters are just looking for more money

5. Hiring Trainees is easier

6. Recruiters are flaky

7. If Recruiters are good they don't leave

8. Recruiters don't want to do BD

9. Anyone I offer will just get countered more and
won't join anyway

10. I need £200K billers

* * * ALERT * * *

ADOPTING AND ACTING UPON THE FOLLOWING BELIEFS MAY SEVERELY INCREASE YOUR WELL BEING AND PROFITS.

THE TEN BELIEFS OF HIGH PERFORMING AGENCY LEADERS

1. Good Recruiters are out there–I just need to target them and engage them.

2. There are good and bad Recruiters everywhere–I will repel the bad and attract the good.

3. Experienced hires will adapt in my team because I will recruit the right type of person for our culture, lay out clear objectives and make their transition easy for them.

4. Money rarely motivates Recruiters to look for a new role but I will be commercially minded and make the people I like the best offer I can to grow my business.

5. Recruiting Trainees is hard work and a major investment; I will recruit experienced Recruiters where possible as they represent less risk. When I have enough critical mass I can build a Graduate / Trainee strategy around my seniors.

6. Some Recruiters are flaky, some aren't. My recruitment process will sort them for me.

7. Good Recruiters can and do leave.

8. Good Recruiters will do BD but will do more when it's managed properly.

9. All good Recruiters will get countered–I have a plan to manage that to minimise any disappointment.

10. I need good people with proven ability to recruit and the right attitude for my business. Anyone that bills over £100K is worthy of consideration.

CONCLUSION

Ok so by now you should have had a few "aha" moments.

Nothing earth shattering because you and I both know that this really isn't difficult, but you should be starting to see where a shift in perspective needs to happen. Maybe you're now realising how tangled up you are in that bubble of yours.

You're not alone. It happens to the best of us on a regular basis. That's why we need each other to gain perspective, share ideas and have a reset.

If you have felt that shift in perspective already then you know that the solution now lies in setting a new course of action.

And hopefully, best of all, you are also feeling a little excited that maybe this isn't as difficult as thought.

That maybe there is a way to release this strangle hold on your business.

So we're going to move into the planning and implementation stage now.

I promise to tone down the tough love now and start sharing the good stuff.

Now we've busted all those myths that are holding you back let's reset with what you should be doing instead.

If as a result of the process I share with you, you just landed your team one more good biller – would it be worth it?

To go all Jerry Maguire for a moment I need you to "help me to help you".

Can you do that?

Because to get onto the good stuff; to steal my secrets and act on the plans I will share with you requires a total commitment.

The good news? It's easier than you think.

Next we're going to look at the component parts of your new talent attraction strategy and break them down so that you can create a clear plan for your business.

PART TWO

CHAPTER 4

IT'S A MARRIAGE NOT A ONE-NIGHT STAND

Before we even begin to think about laying out your seriously effective talent attraction strategy I want to share the psychology behind the system with you.

Everything you do; from deciding how to talk about your vacancy through to making an offer and managing your new team member's induction; must be done in a way that speaks to the **mindset** of the **right type** of Recruiter.

Your right type of Recruiter is not necessarily anyone else's.

But whatever defines your ideal recruit, I know you definitely want the type of Recruiter that will stay and add value to your business long-term. The type of Recruiter that lives and breathes your values. The type of Recruiter you can trust.

Everything you do in your attraction strategy should be based on attracting people with similar or complimenting values for your firm.

The people you attract should feel a deep connection to your core values. And what you offer must allay their fears about a move and amplify their excitement about their future with you.

This is where many recruitment leaders go wrong. They don't spend enough time examining whether this potential new hire is right for them long-term or ensuring the candidates buys in and it costs them dearly – either through rushed hires that fail or repelling the very candidates they want to attract.

It's easy to do. If you're busy with a to-do list as long as your arm and you're feeling the pressure of that vacant desk; it's easy to rush towards a potential solution. With the added belief that good people are hard to find; and even average people being hard to land; it's no wonder so many leaders just like you end up with a hire they regret.

So where does this disconnect happen? How can you fix it? How do you get into the candidate's mindset and attract them to your brand but still screen them properly to ensure they're a good fit?

It starts with the candidate mindset. If you can understand how a Recruiter typically thinks both before, during and after an interview you can ensure your process wins them over, keeps them engaged and results in a successful hire.

The vast majority of recruitment firms either don't understand this or don't care and it leads to a pretty poor candidate experience.

By far, the biggest complaint that experienced hires have about interviewing with new firms is that the interview is too one-sided and feels like an interrogation and that the interviewer expects lots of detail from the candidate but won't offer the same in return.

I get it, I do. The majority of agency owners and leaders have had their fingers burnt.

Have you?

If you have then I totally understand why you might be a little cynical initially, why you might not believe what they tell you, why you feel the need to question and challenge them. I get it, I do. But it's not the answer.

I have the answer. The winning formula for understanding how you need to engage with your ideal candidate. There are many levels to this engagement with the ultimate and most powerful being the face-to-face interview. But if you understand the basic sucess formula and adopt it you will see that it threads through everything… your careers page, your videos, your social strategy, your email campaigns. Everything.

This is the answer:

BUILD A BOND + FIND PAIN + SHOW EMPATHY + AGITATE PAIN
+ OFFER SOLUTION + BRAND NEW DAY + PROOF

SCENARIO BASED INTERVIEWING

We're going to come back to this later and I am going to give you an easy way to build interview plans around this formula. Let me give you the overview now.

BUILDING A BOND

Before you do anything else you must build rapport and create a bond with your potential candidate. You must be likeable and trustworthy. If you really want to find out who the real candidate is they need to like and trust you or they won't step forward and they won't engage. Not properly. I know you can do this, you have this skill, you use it all the time with candidates and clients for your agency.

FIND THEIR PAIN

Once you have established some trust your potential hire is far more likely to be honest and reveal their real personality. Before you go any further you must expose their pain because later on you will need to sell your "solution" as an employer. Finding their pain is never as straightforward as asking directly. Quite often there is more than one reason offered and it will be masked with a reason they think sounds good in interview. Your job is to expose the core source of pain and understand how this makes them feel.

SHOWING EMPATHY

Once you identify where their pain is you must show empathy. And if you are super smart you will have a personal story to share that will deepen your bond and show them you really understand on a meaningful level. Sharing a story here will buy you so much credibility and will prepare them for what comes next. You must never forget that the only reason they are even meeting with you is probably because they feel undervalued, misunderstood or unrecognised in some way. So speak to that and share your own personal experiences and feelings.

AGITATE THEIR PAIN

This sounds a bit cruel I know. But it is essential that once you have broken down where their pain is and have shown empathy you must agitate that pain by asking them what happens if this isn't resolved or doesn't change? How will they feel then? What will they lose?

Making them face the abyss of their misery or frustration will amplify their desire for a solution and an escape. You must do this before offering them the solution. Because you have taken the time to understand their source of pain you will know which specific features and benefits of joining your team to present and focus on.

BRAND NEW DAY

This is where you create a vision for how their life, and most importantly how they feel about it, will change by joining your team. It's important that you are descriptive and specific. This better, more colourful, happier version of their current life is what they will achieve by joining your company.

PROOF

Once you have developed a bond and gained their trust, exposed their pain and shown empathy by sharing some personal stories, agitated their pain to amplify their desire for change and then created a compelling vision for their new start you must then finish with some proof. Proof of how you or people in your team have achieved similar transformations.

All well and good yes? But I hear you.... you're thinking "all well and good Tara but what if they're rubbish and I'm effectively doing all this without knowing if they're good or not?".

You're still going to assess and screen this candidate and you're going to do it using scenario based interview questions (more on that later) – but you do it AFTER you make them fall in love with your firm not BEFORE. And this is where almost everyone goes wrong. If you get this right every candidate that meets you will fall in love with your company and any other interviews will pale into insignificance by comparison. Ultimately, your aim is for them to leave wanting to be a part of your team.

If you take the time to make them relax and trust you, then you will be far more likely to expose the real person in front of you; and as a result it will be easier to assess whether they are the right person for your business.

So what if they turn out not to be right for you?

It's never going to hurt your company to have people wanting to come and work for you even if you don't want them. As long as you manage it in the right way anyway. There's just too many upsides to working this way to ignore it. You're far more likely to engage each candidate, and create greater feel good factor about your brand as people go back out into the world with a great impression.

You will also find that because people have had a good experience they show you who they really are, so if you do offer them employ-ment your probability of long-term success with this hire is far greater.

So rest assured, flipping your usual strategy will only bring you better results.

You have to be realistic. You really can't keep waiting for that awesome candidate to waltz into your office begging you for the chance to learn from you; it's not going to happen in today's market. You must adapt. Your business can only survive and thrive if you continually attract the best people. This is the one thing your business cannot live without. So just do it.

You know this will work. You operate a version of this with client visits, perhaps not quite so structured, but then most of your indi-vidual clients don't generate as much in profit for your business as a great new team member. But it is pretty similar. You go and meet a new client seeing all the potential. You go in to win them over from the start; you anticipate their concerns and objections so that you are prepared; you bond; you build rapport; you probe and gather facts; you ask for the business; you answer fears (objections and you close for what you want. All the while you are judging and assessing whether you can work in the way that you want to, and you're managing their expectations so that you both get what you need. It's really not so different when it comes to interviewing.

I know it's a different way of thinking. I get it might be a bit more uncomfortable at first but I have some great tools I can share at the end of this book to help you practice and implement this.

Unless your business is awash with great Recruiters lining up to join your team then I need you to be brave. I need you to throw away what you already have and start again and make sure everything in your process is built with your perfect candidate in mind.

If you don't build your strategy around their mindset instead of yours, the game is lost from the start.

This idea of getting into the mindset of the people you need, instead of waiting for them to adopt yours is one that transformed my career.

It's a really powerful lesson that I actually learned many years ago. It wasn't initially about internal recruitment but it made a lasting impression and heavily influenced both how I targeted, interviewed and managed my teams from there on in. I have simply refined this further over the years of leading my business in the world of Rec2Rec so I'm going to share it with you.

The night I decided to resign

I had this particular light bulb moment many years ago when I was still fairly new to management (I'm talking c2001) and I was tearing my hair out as to why some of my Consultants didn't seem to care about their results, why they weren't working as hard as me, why they were fighting me all the time. It was starting to feel very personal and I knew it was bringing out the worst in me as a Manager. The very typical, "big biller gets promoted to manager and then loses it" story.

Luckily for me I reached a turning point when one night, while tearing my hair out and pacing the floor of my living room ranting and dramatically declaring I was done with being a manager to my partner (now husband and yes also in recruitment) I actually said the words "that's it I'm done, I'm resigning".

My husband is physically a really big guy and he had been very patiently listening to my long list of moans and groans. Following my declaration he very calmly stood up, walked over to me, put his arms around and whispered in my ear..."shut the f*ck up".

He's actually a lovely guy I promise and what he went on to highlight to me was that my expectations were unreasonable. He reminded me that my influencing skills, when applied to clients and candidates, were great. That there wasn't a client or candidate I couldn't convert because I always questioned, listened and then sold them the solution, showing empathy all along the way. I then championed them until they got what they came to me for.

I hadn't been applying the same approach to my team.

I was going in with way too much expectation. I just expected them to "get it" and do as asked. Fear of failure was creating pressure and in turn the wrong behaviours from me. And, when they obviously resisted, I was taking it personally.

I would never take such an approach to a client.

I can remember staring out of the window while the dots connected and realised that annoyingly he was right. When dealing with clients or candidates I would always enter into a relationship with the approach that I must absolutely listen to what they need, probe around their pain, surface their fears and concerns, show them how I can help but firmly lay down the boundaries of what a good relationship with me looks like, and then gain their commitment to a very specific course of action - all of which was delivered in a friendly, professional and empathic way.

I had it down pat.

But for some reason I was throwing this away when I dealt with my team.

So the uncomfortable truth was this was all on me.

If I took responsibility for the problem I could own the result.

So I had to stop blaming them and look at making some changes.

For some reason I was imposing unrealistic expectations on how they should think, respond and act. As soon as I changed my mindset on this and started to treat my team as if they were clients, everything changed.

I realised by job as a Manager was still sales / business development / client relationship management, whatever you want to call it.

My job now as a Manager was to be on sales mode full time. Just internally with my team.

I had to constantly rinse and repeat my old client format of listening, probing, surfacing pain, showing the solution, setting boundaries and expectations and then working hard to support their goals.

It would need to change how I talked to them, how I structured meetings, how I managed feedback and how I motivated them.

As soon as I saw them as clients, and new hires as new clients, everything changed for me.

I really cannot express how much this moment changed my career. Literally the day after this everything changed for me.

This skill served me well over the years as a leader and it is a skill I had no choice but to hone further out of necessity when I set up Recruiter Republic. Every single person I met was a Recruiter that thought they knew how I should do my job for them and usually they were way off. They were by far the most complex candidates I have ever worked with and I had to reset everything I knew about recruitment.

I had no choice but to question them, listen to them and package up the solution for them. If I didn't, I had no business.

You may have come to the same realisation as I did, but in my experience that would put you in a very small group of people, it's rare that I meet anyone that has applied this mindset to attracting their teams.

When it comes to your internal recruitment strategy are you applying the same strategy you would with a client or candidate to connect, build rapport, surface fear and pain, show the solution and set expectations? Are you making the potential candidate feel good about you, your company and the experience of meeting you or not?

Forget what you think they should do or feel or what you think they should be motivated to do, that comes later. How are you making them feel with your advertising, your careers page, your initial conversations and meetings? Are you attracting your ideal candidate or repelling them?

Are you making them fall in love with your brand or scaring them?

Do you make them feel good or make them feel bad?

Are you maybe setting unrealistic expectations?

You see, you can't see a potential Recruiter as the enemy. You can't go in expecting them to be bad.

And I know that sounds obvious but you might not even be aware that you're making it look that way.

Equally you can't afford to go the other way and do a wishy washy light touch interview for fear of scaring them off. You'll never get to the good stuff that buys them in for the right reasons.

Your aim should be that **every** person you meet leaves saying great things about your firm. They should be a promoter not a detractor whether you want to progress with them or not. There's a way to let them down gently and treat them well if they're not right and a way to make them feel good if they are.

But more importantly, if you can connect with the people you are interviewing in a more meaningful way, for a more long-term fit in terms of compatibility, you will not only convert more of them to join you but you will have far greater ability to grow more rapidly and protect the core DNA that makes your business unique.

Quick exercise for you.

Think back to the last few people you have interviewed. If you could replay that interview; with what I have just said in mind; can you see my point?

Who meets them first? Please tell me it's you... the absolute best person in the company to promote and sell your vision? OR someone equally as skilled at least?

Can you see what might be wrong already? Because you have a lack of belief in your ability to meet good candidates are you delegating initial interviews to someone else? Someone less capable than you of selling your company? Less capable at understanding someone's potential? Someone less able to build rapport?

As we break down the system into stages please know that each element is designed to attract the right people, repel the wrong ones, surface their pain, show them your solution, set expectations and seek a commitment.

The system is designed to take care of their core fears when it comes to exploring new opportunities and take away their excuses to stay put in a role that does not fulfil them.

They will opt in or opt out on that basis.

The right ones opt in.

TAKE-AWAYS

1. Your target candidate's mindset has to be understood before you meet them as it needs to influence all of your branding, advertising and early stages of the attraction process.

2. When you meet you focus on BONDING and gaining their trust.

3. You must discover where they are in PAIN.

4. You must show EMPATHY and share PERSONAL stories.

5. You must agitate their PAIN and make them face the future as it would be if they don't change their circumstances.

6. You must offer them the specific SOLUTIONS they will find by joining your team.

7. You need to create a vision of their BRAND NEW DAY and how that will make them FEEL.

8. You need to give them PROOF by showing them examples of others who have achieved transformation.

9. Only once all this is done do you screen and assess using scenario based interviewing–more on that later.

10. Your aim is to give EVERY person a great experience and make EVERY person want to join your team whether they are right or not.

11. You ONLY pick the people you BELIEVE in.

CHAPTER 5

YOUR HEROES & VILLAINS

Before you meet any potential new team members you must first decide what makes your company so great to work for, the ideal people to attract (we're going to call them your heroes) and the people you wish to repel (we'll call them your villains).

Much like most online daters promote the qualities in themselves they think their ideal partner will be attracted to, you must do the same. Equally you must repel the people that would be wrong for you.

Please don't skip over this part (I know how impatient you probably feel) but I assure you that everything that comes after this part will fail if you don't take the time to think this through.

For your talent strategy to be successful long-term it should be unique to you and your team or company and it should be made up of a series of steps that everybody understands and recognises.

All well and good, but it has to be underpinned by a well-defined proposition. And once your process is built it must be anchored into your business by training EVERYONE that is involved in the process.

Ultimately, the foundation on which your talent attraction process will be built lies in your ability to clearly answer these questions...

WHY WOULD YOUR "HERO" WANT TO COME AND JOIN YOUR TEAM? AND WHY WOULD YOUR VILLAIN AVOID IT?

You'd be amazed at how many recruitment leaders I meet that haven't defined their ideal candidate (hero), although they normally have pretty strong ideas about what doesn't work for them (their villain).

And even fewer have a clearly defined idea of what would attract their heroes or repel their villains and until this is done you'll never be in control of the quality of candidates you meet.

So how do you do this?

DEFINING YOUR HERO

Let's start with your ideal candidate.

You will probably be able to define some overarching qualities that are relevant to all new hires and some separate qualities that are unique to each specific vacancy you are looking to fill.

But what are they? Do you even know what they are? Could your wider team explain them in a compelling and consistent way? Give yourself a break if you realise you've got a glaring gap here–most firms do.

But think about it. If you can't define the ideal Recruiter for your team how on earth do you communicate that to world and expect people to identify and be attracted?

Let's start with some of the key qualities of your company as an employer.

Make some notes here about what key features (and benefits) apply to your working environment, team dynamic, processes, tools, location, training, working style, benefits, rewards and sector focus. We're going to link them to your ideal candidate in a moment.

Notes

Now you've made some notes, let's go through a really simple, but effective, exercise to show you the questions you need to ask. As you ask and answer these questions you need to consider the key benefits or advantages to working for your firm and who your hero needs to be to find those things an advantage.

Examples

Your location is outskirts of a city. Your hero lives outside and hates battling commuter traffic everyday...that person will LOVE your location.

If your client base or nature of your specific niche requires high-touch face to face consultation with clients and candidates then the type of candidate who will LOVE this is probably compromised in their current role and is denied the chance to work this way.

These are just example questions to get you started – feel free to elaborate and add to the list.

Killer Hero Questions

- Where do they live?

- What experience do they have?

- What should they enjoy doing?

- Which particular skills will they have?

- What would they like to learn or become better at?

- What are their medium to long-term ambitions?

- What do they wish they had more of?

- What would they change if they could?

- Which words would they use to describe themselves?

Example:

- London – or commutable to City within 45 mins

- Minimum 12 months in recruitment – any perm desk

- Love candidate networking and meetings

- Strong use of LinkedIn, producing mailshots, creating content and events

- Advanced negotiation techniques and able to win retainers

- Lead a team of their own

- More headroom, less KPI management, a voice in the business

- Better tools, involvements in recruiting trainees

- Confident, professional, solution orientated

DEFINING YOUR VILLAIN

Once again, as you follow the same format as we did when we defined your hero, you will find you have some qualities that are relevant to all candidates and others that are specific to each opportunity with your team.

Let's repeat the exercise but this time think about the type of candidate that would NOT be right for your team and would be very likely to fail.

Killer Villain Questions:

- Where do they live?

- What experience do they lack?

- What do they dislike doing?

- Which particular skills will they lack?

- What are their medium to long-term ambitions?

- What do they wish they had more of?

- What would they change if they could?

- Which words would they use to describe themselves

Example:

- Commuting in more than an hour

- No face-to-face meetings / BD / registrations

- Making proactive calls

- Self-management, closing sales, candidate control

- Launch own agency

- Advertising, job boards, holiday

- People around them–quite critical

- Clever, independent, maverick

Are you starting to form a picture here?

Great – hold onto it – we're coming back to it shortly.

DEFINING YOUR HEROES & VILLAINS

Identifying what you seek in the ideal candidate (hero or what you don't want (your villain) is only half the battle.

To create compelling adverts, content, videos or even just a robust interview plan requires you to link the qualities you want to attract or repel and link them to key features of your employment offering – or in HR speak – your employer value proposition.

This is where you wrap up your pitch to speak to the ideal candidate's pain, articulate the value to them of the solutions you provide as an employer and the resulting experience they will have. This is where you paint a picture of the bright new day they will have when they join your team. It should also completely repel the villain.

If you think about how the ideal candidate will be in pain with their current employer you will probably be hard-pressed to come up with more than five to seven key points – any more than this and you'll bore both yourself and them or just confuse them.

Don't worry this isn't an exhaustive exercise and it will only need a tweak on one or two points to tailor to suit each individual role you have. And remember you shouldn't have more than five to seven points here. This builds a framework for your value proposition and it's not a list of EVERYTHING you seek – it's the key and most valuable points.

So you can go ahead and start thinking and make notes now just to get you started. At this point I just want you to start thinking so this sinks in properly.

Go ahead and note down each area of pain your *ideal* candidate probably feels in their current role in order to find your opportunity attractive.

Example...Your ideal candidate NEEDS to be capable of working independently as you are still an active biller yourself and won't have the time to constantly coach them (and no you can't say it like that in an interview which is what most people do!).

For you to achieve this you will need to seek qualities in someone such as a proactive nature, ability to think independently, being solution oriented and an ability to prioritise daily workloads.

For a candidate to have those qualities specifically yet be in pain they would need to feel over-managed or suffocated where they are now with little freedom to make their own decisions.

If their pain is caused by being over-managed and that makes them feel suffocated or patronised then think about how you can empathise with that, I'm sure you can think of an empathy story for that...maybe a time when your ex-boss would drive you mad with constant chasing up and following up to the point that there wasn't any time to do the very thing they were chasing you up about!

Next, think about how that frustration will grow over time. You can then create your "brand new day" vision for them around being independent, feeling free and working with trust from the start.

Do you see how this works? Use your ideal candidate qualities to work backwards to identify their potential areas of pain – it's quite straight forward to then create your empathy stories, amplify their pain, and create their brand-new day around that point.

ATTRACTING YOUR HERO

So whether you are attracting your hero via advertising, direct approach, introduction from a Rec2Rec agency or staff referral, you will attract your hero to your brand in exactly the same way.

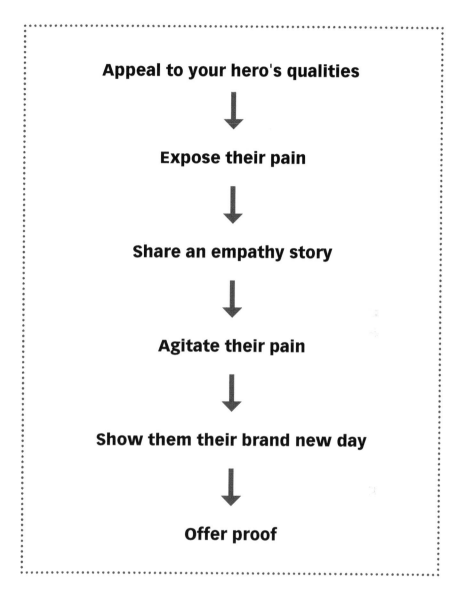

If you create sets of these for the typical hero qualities you seek then you can re-use, rotate and re-theme your marketing all the time.

Now you understand the process you can do the same for your villain.

REPELLING YOUR VILLAIN

We're not going to use this as much as your hero attraction strategy and the way that we use this will be more subtle but it's important we do have it ready. You will run a very similar process but this time instead of an empathy story you have an exclusion story.

Repel your villain's qualities

⬇

Expose their pain

⬇

Share an exclusion story

⬇

Agitate their pain

⬇

Brand new nightmare

⬇

Proof why it won't work

It's a similar process as before – we identify the qualities of our villain and then the pain they feel in their current role, we exclude YOUR role by ensuring they focus on a key feature that will only agitate their pain further so that we can send them away and should they still hang around we will have some proof of how someone similar found your role or company totally wrong so you can turn them away or reject them as a favour to them. **Remember – nobody should leave feeling bad or rejected.**

Example:

Let's imagine one of your villain qualities is them being "selfish". You know the type, someone that prefers to put their own needs ahead of the team. In fact they do so to the extent that it can often hurt the team.

An area of pain the villain may feel in their current firm might be around rules around sharing candidates and leads and any penalties of not doing so.

Your exclusion story should be around how you so actively promote team collaboration that it has been made impossible to hide candidates or clients because of how your CRM works.

You agitate their pain further by showing them how your team is so committed to team work that 90% of your placements are split fees and all vacancies and candidates are open to the wider team at all times. This should be enough for them to deselect themselves – if not then your nightmare proof can be an example of someone who tried to circumnavigate the system and lost.

Run through the key qualities of your villain here and list out every-thing they would NOT like about your firm but your HERO would.

Is this starting to make sense?

It's really important that you have a clear view on your hero and villain and their associated qualities.

When their definitions are front and centre it will make all of your attraction strategies much stronger, it will be far harder to let the wrong candidate through your process and you will achieve much higher levels of engagement from heroes and self opt-outs by your villains.

What's also really easy for you; is that once you have defined them you can ensure everyone in your team understands them and knows what to look for and avoid.

It's amazing how much easier it is to find what you want when you focus on it.

It will make all of your marketing so much more powerful. It will be polarizing - but that's ok.

You see up until now, in your bid to keep all options open, to avoid having all your eggs in one basket, and to avoid isolating a potential candidate in a pool severely short of talent, you have unknowingly made your option almost invisible. It's so beige, so vanilla, and so middle of the road that it doesn't "speak" to anyone in particular. Your job adverts and marketing strategies look the same as the many others.

You have to treat your target people as consumers and consumers respond to adverts, communications, recommendations and content based on how they FEEL.

You need your hero to identify with what you stand for and how you work. You want them to feel understood because you have empathy for their pain and your own war stories to share. People like being around people that understand them. We're all looking for our tribe–both at work and in our personal life.

You absolutely want your hero to fall in love with your solutions and the vision of their future with you and that can't happen unless they really connect with your values.

Is this starting to make sense?

Equally, you need your villain to opt themselves out early. Let them clog up someone else's diary.

This theory of heroes and villains came to me in the first year of launching Recruiter Republic. I had, until that point, considered myself a pretty strong content producer and I certainly knew how to write a good job advert. But nothing I was producing was getting results. No job board adverts worked (but then we know good Recruiters will rarely apply to adverts anyway), while email marketing was getting ridiculously low response rates and social posts were meeting silence. I've got to admit that my ego was a little bruised. I had been Group Digital Director at Hays in UK for goodness sake – in charge of strategy and major multi-million pound budgets and here I was struggling to rewrite a job advert that converted!

I was experiencing the same issue you are now. What works in all so many other areas of recruitment fails when it comes to attracting Recruiters.

I can remember sitting in my office in Stockholm at the time and feeling particularly stubborn...I spent several hours redrafting adverts, comparing to others online but still couldn't see what else to do.

That is until, out of sheer desperation, I called quite a few Recruiters I knew. Once the first two calls raised some interesting points I was on a roll and I must have called over 20 people that day, some that had worked for me in the past, some trusted placements and also some completely new candidates.

Each and every person had pretty much the same feedback and by the way the feedback was for recruitment adverts generally – including mine. Here were the main feedback points:

- The adverts all sounded the same

- They didn't believe what the adverts said

- None of them told them anything they really wanted to know

- They were so used to this being the case they weren't really reading them anymore

- They didn't trust that any enquiry would be treated confidentially

I can't pretend the answers came overnight. I experimented with how to write adverts and email copy for several months, I also spent a lot of money studying copywriting, split testing and more.

Finally, somewhere around six months or so after having my light bulb moment about why the adverts weren't working I finally had my second light bulb moment on how to write them differently.

The proof? Well I guess the fact that I have managed to build a successful Rec2Rec agency, an award winning one no less (and yes I'm bloody proud of that – it's something few others have managed to do), might be seen as some proof of this. But the real proof? The many, many emails and LinkedIn messages my team get from Recruiters stating how refreshing our approaches are, how compelling the messaging is, how they feel we must really know the company well…that's what tells me it's working. Where there was silence (or on occasion even mock outrage) there was now open dialogue, feedback, connection and results.

People felt I understood their challenges, sympathised with their situation, that I "got it". And because I didn't oversell jobs and fill the text with fluff, they trusted what I said a lot more. It had more power. We started getting far less poor quality responses (villains) and far more high quality responses (heroes).

It was only in my need to try and explain how to do this to some of my inner circle clients that this analogy formed.

CHAPTER 6

IT'S ALL ABOUT
THE FUNNEL

We all recognise that the biggest inhibitor to your ultimate success is lack of incoming talent. But what should the solution look like?

I am going to give you a sneak-peak here of your talent strategy and what it will look like as a process. But I do so now NOT for you to try and rush ahead and miss some very crucial points – instead I do so to help you understand how it must always be "on".

Let me explain…

Your problem is both quantity and quality. And you likely recruit in fits and starts. Flurries of activity when the need is urgent and then nothing until the next resignation or surge in workload. The problem with this is it limits you to only ever accessing the candidates that are looking to make a move NOW (remember that 4% we talked about?). And it limits you most of the time to only the quality of candidate that is willing to apply online or heaven forbid put their CV online.

To be successful long term, to have the pick of the best candidates, requires you to have a constant attraction strategy in play. Now before you panic it doesn't have to be exhaustive and there are easy ways to automate parts of the process. But just as a quick reminder here's why you need to be "on" all the time.

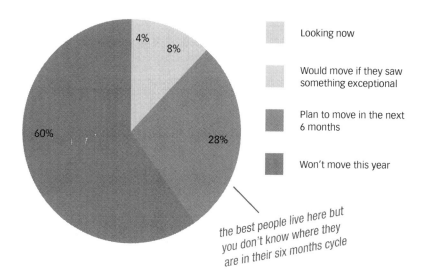

Looking now

Would move if they saw something exceptional

Plan to move in the next 6 months

Won't move this year

the best people live here but you don't know where they are in their six months cycle

If you switch on and off you only ever access the 4% MAXIMUM of your local pool of recruiters that are actively seeking a new role (and I can tell you now that 4% is VERY active and is swamped with choices), your chances of both getting the quality you seek and actually landing them are extremely slim.

But what about the additional 8% that would consider a move if it was "right" and the 28% who plan to move within the next six months? They aren't applying, and they definitely don't have their CV online but they are feeling "pain". If you can nurture these candidates on an ongoing basis when they do connect with your messaging or when they do reach the decision to move within the following six months you will be an obvious choice for them.

Not only will this ensure you have more candidates, but these candidates will have the added benefit of not having quite so many options to keep them busy, plus they will be primed for your opportunity already.

So once your attraction funnel is "on" it stays "on", ok?

HERE'S WHAT IT LOOKS LIKE

Now that you have identified your heroes and villains, and got into the mindset of the candidates you really need so that you can communicate with them in a highly effective way, and *(maybe grudgingly)* accepted that this machine stays on at all times, all that is left is to map out each stage of the process above.

Each stage keeps in mind the candidate mindset, speaks to your hero and repels your villain. Once you have this process nailed it should be trained across the whole team so that it is universally understood and common language is used. This will become your normal, I promise and I have lots of tools to help you to implement this later on.

CHAPTER 7

7 STEPS TO BECOMING A TALENT MAGNET

STEP #1–ATTRACTION PROCESS

To attract your heroes you must gain their attention. You must break their pattern of thinking and connect. This can't just be about pushing jobs on people. Your attraction strategy must be made up of a blend of activities across a range of channels – all driving the right people to your careers page (if you don't have one get one), where you can create time and space to appeal to your hero. To give them the time and space to like and trust you. To make them fall in love with your brand.

While the various routes to your careers page can and should vary and the style of the advert or post that attracts their attention can be different – the main hub of information, that compelling content that attracts your hero, stays the same and should be hosted on your careers page.

Your ideal blueprint should look something like this:

CAREER PAGES

You will see a major proportion of the channels used are social. While you can and should retain traffic coming from job adverts (print or online) and converting general website visits, the reality is that 8% and 28% will come from social network platforms and no, not just Linkedin.

Don't even think about dismissing these other channels. The entire population of Recruiters you want to attract are connected to the Internet 24 hours per day. And according to various online reports:

- 50% of Recruiter's on-line time is on a social network.

- On average people have five social media accounts

- They spend 24 hours a day within 2 feet of at least 1 mobile device.

- During the course of a day they use on average 3 separate devices.

You have to go where they go and you have to communicate with them in the context of the channel you use at the time.

There's literally no point posting adverts out on sites that they won't visit and just stubbornly wait for them to find you. You must go where they are.

Please don't make the same mistake that so many other recruitment business leaders do, wasting time and money on "fudgy" adverts that will only ever be found by the 4%. Go where the high-value 36% are and gain their attention instead.

Now before you embark on a flurry of content creation for these channels or for your careers page I want you to think about how this should work.

Don't over complicate this. In fact, just take a moment to think about how you interact with brands that attract you. How often do you respond to a direct advert for a service or product and instantly purchase something from an unknown company? Particularly a new brand out of the blue promoting a product?

If you're like most other people then the answer is; rarely. Unless of course you already had a defined need and even if you did you probably had a brand you already trusted that you deferred to first.

But if you think about a time you have bought something online or scheduled a consultation or asked for a quote it probably wasn't in response to an advert for a direct product – it was probably because someone you know recommended them, or they produced something of value that you liked. Perhaps that golfing brand offered you a video on how to improve your handicap? Perhaps that new make-up brand you purchased from offered you a free contouring video first? Either way I bet you had a period where they gave you something, engaged with you, got you to like and trust them before they asked for the sale.

The same applies to the Recruiters that you are trying to target. Unless they are in that 4% of Recruiters that are actively applying for roles then your ideal candidate is not going to just respond to an advert.

You must use multiple channels and a series of touch points to get them to trust and like you. And then, and only then, are you likely to gain their attention in a meaningful way. So, your content must do that – build both like and trust. Be useful. DO NOT hit them constantly with job adverts. It doesn't work.

You want that 8% that would move for the right thing, and the 28% that plan to move in the next six months to spend time with you and fall in love with your brand.

And because a lot of this content will be offered in a way that they like and allows them to self-serve the information they need, you won't scare them away.

In fact, as you layer up these touch points, using lots of different strategies and with a smart semi-automated system, they will convert themselves.

Think about it. If they're planning to move in the next six months, and you put this system into your business, within six months maximum you will see placements dropping on a regular basis. And more importantly they are already primed and excited about your brand AND they probably haven't taken any other steps yet.

So here's your shopping list to build out your attraction funnel.

- Build a careers @ Facebook page if you don't have one already

- Build a life@ Instagram page if you don't have one already

- Build a careers@ Twitter page if you don't have one already

- Build a Careers page on your company LinkedIn Page

- Build a website careers page if you don't have one already

- Create vacancy advert templates for your common key hires using hero qualities to attract

- Create an opt-in pop up for your careers page to collect visitor email addresses

- Set up an email autoresponder service to collect emails and automate regular emails to build rapport with your career page visitors

Now don't worry if you are new to this and haven't done this before. At the back of this book I have a lot of resources to help you through each of these stages if you haven't done this before. If you have some of these already in place then I have a checklist to make sure what you have is actually what you need and if needed you can follow the checklist to improve what you have. For those of you that need to set up these processes from scratch check out our workshops that you can attend to help get you started (details in Part 3)

Once you have this basic infrastructure in place then you can start adding content and by far the highest converting is video.

Content themes should speak to your candidate's pain, which you have already identified. These could be:

- Day in the life videos

- Snap-shots of things you're doing

- Clips of rewards

- Desks shots

- Interviews and Q&As with leaders in your business

- Consultant bios

- A virtual tour of the office

- A deep dive into some of your rewards and benefits

- A docu-series about your training.

Content themes should speak to your candidate's pain, which you have already identified. These could be day in the life videos, snapshots of things you're doing, clips of rewards, desks shots, interviews and Q&As with leaders in your business, or Consultants, a tour of the office, a deep dive into some of your rewards and benefits, a docu-series about your training.

Brainstorm some initial ideas here but do refer back to your candidate's pain first as you want to ensure you have some strong content that speaks to their pain and demonstrates proof of their brand-new day!

Don't go light here. You need lots of different items of content so that people revisit your pages.

Why?

Do you know how many interactions it takes for the average consumer to start to like and trust a brand?

Nine (at time of writing anyway).

And in a market where you have cynical and fearful Recruiters it is probably much higher for you.

So take nine as the minimum.

A potential candidate needs to engage with your brand nine times before they will take an approach seriously or like and trust you enough to talk to you.

And no, that doesn't mean nine clumsy inmails with a template job posting.

If you use all channels available to you, share content that speaks to your heroes and repels your villains, and keep your attraction machine "on", you will expand your audience for the usual 3-4% to a whopping 40%.

You will also save time on wasted interviews with poor quality candidates that currently clogging up your system.

You have 5 seconds to hold someone's attention (*yes we humans in the digital age now offically have a shorter attention span than a goldfish*) – GRAB IT and make the first 5 seconds of any ad / video / copy have an impact.

CHAPTER 8

UNCLOGGING YOUR RECRUITMENT MACHINE

So now you have totally got into the mindset of your ideal candidate and understand who your heroes and villains are. You have also strengthened the activities to bring potential candidates into your attraction machine - what's important now is that you also have a robust filter (because even though you will try hard to repel the villains they have a habit of turning up anyway).

Much like that expensive vacuum cleaner would stop working if it had no filter, you too must ensure your recruitment machine does not get clogged up with villains. Filtering and assessing candidates as they come into your machine as a result of your many attraction strategies is essential. But the question is how do you do this without repelling the good people?

How do you keep the ones you like in process before you know you like them? How you do assess to ensure you don't waste your time but still make it feel good to the candidate?

Because it does need to feel good...to every single person you attract without fail.

Let me introduce you to the ultimate assessment process. It's easy as **ABC** and It looks like this:

ASSESS

To initially assess your candidate you must speak to them.

This is **NOT** a telephone interview – don't call it that. EVER. Candidates hate it. Instead offer the chat as if it is for their benefit.

But you do want to get to know your candidate and understand whether it's worth it for both of you to meet.

You should assess them based on Hero Qualities (I have a template for you later on), Likability and Emotional Intelligence.

Their Hero Quality score (or HQS) is literally how well they measure up against your desired qualities.

Likability is how engaging they are on the phone (they will after all be doing this every day for their job with you), if they can't be engaging about themselves they have no chance when it comes to their vacancies or candidates.

Emotional Intelligence is simply measured by how well they interpret your questions and use the information you give them to be compelling.

It really doesn't need to be more complicated than that. Too many people go straight into interrogation mode and put people off OR just ask about their current desk and billings and book someone straight in for interview which does nothing to tell you whether they're your type of person and does nothing to motivate them to actually attend the interview if offered.

If you decide that your candidate scores well they progress to B. If they don't, you very nicely reject them using their own stated desires (i.e. If you know you need someone to work independently as the team you are recruiting for has a busy perms manager then someone who appears to lack confidence in this area can be rejected nicely without feeling rejected).

If you decide they are not strong enough then you simply tell them that right now you absolutely cannot do the wrong thing by them by trying to progress this just because you like them when you know full well it's not what they want or need right not. Annoying as that is.

You simply let them know that you would very much like to stay in touch as you anticipate that another option may well become available in the coming months where the leader will have more available time for coaching and mentoring. Agree to stay in touch for that type of option.

Nobody likes to be rejected. And nobody hates it more than a Recruiter. So don't make it sound as if they are. Make it sound like you're doing them a favour and you'll win their loyalty and respect. You'll also be much more likely to gain a promoter than a detractor.

BUILD

This is to **build** rapport.; **build** proof of solutions for their pain and **build** a vision of their brand new day. This is their motivation to come and meet you. So once you have asked enough questions to assess them and decide that you like them;

it's essential that you start building rapport on a deeper level. Show empathy for their situation, and share a story too. Start building their confidence that you have specific solutions and share an outline of how their working life and perhaps personal life can be positively impacted by joining your team.

COMMIT

When you have built up rapport, solutions and future vision get them to commit. That doesn't mean a hard sell or a "close". You simply tell them you'd love to meet if they feel what you offer sounds good and feels like a positive move. Tell them you're ready to meet straight away but you only want to do so if they are ready. If they're unsure at all they are free to go and do some further research on you before committing.

TOP TIPS:

1. Use templates for assessing people on the phone.

2. Remember A (**assess**) then if you like them B (**build**), then go for C (**commitment**); they opt in or opt out–there's no convincing anyone.

3. Make them feel good. If they are talking to you it's because they feel unloved, undervalued or misunderstood. Make notes and save them for the actual interview.

4. Follow up immediately. As soon as that commitment is made confirm it immediately.

5. Anyone that you reject is handled graciously, is thanked for their time and is given some encouragement and one piece of practical advice.

CHAPTER 9

"THE ART OF SEDUCTION" A.K.A CANDIDATE ENGAGEMENT

Attracting your heroes and then filtering out the odd villain is a key stage to attracting people into your talent pipeline so it makes sense that once you get them there you make sure they are nurtured and engaged to ensure that stay in process.

Fancy HR types might talk about candidate engagement but what it really boils down to; what you're really here to find out; is how do you keep good candidates on the hook once you've spent hours getting them on the bloody hook in the first place.

Is there anything more annoying than spending weeks looking for people, courting them, managing them through to arrange an interview only for them to go AWOL or flake out last minute? And to add insult to injury do so via text or worse no contact at all????

Sometimes you can't avoid this – it's a common problem when you're only exposed to the 4% of the candidate pool. Sometimes it's your process that's the problem. It's just not robust enough, it's letting people that aren't in enough pain to get into the system or it's just not engaging.

Many a good candidate has fallen into this gap between confirming a meeting and the date of the meeting never to return. They will claim many reasons but what it usually all boils down to is a lack of filtering or too long a gap between making the commitment and the actual date to meet.

In that gap, that costly time lapse, one of the following has usually happened:

1. You've woken them up; primed them for escape and then they've got off the phone all amped up with nowhere to go. Now they're on a roll and if you're not careful they get click happy and start exploring other options. So now you have competition and if they move faster than you – well you might just lose out.

2. In the time lapse between your initial chat and the arranged interview, the FEAR kicks in. Fear of someone finding out, fear that a move represents risk, fear that their earnings will drop, fear that the mortgage they want to go for will fail, fear that they will have a bad interview experience, fear that they will be put under pressure before they are ready. FEAR! FEAR! FEAR! Recruiters are full of fear.

3. They were never serious about a move. If you're good at assessing Recruiters before booking them in you should eliminate this one but every now and then you get one slip through the net. They're career flirts, they are high maintenance and a little needy. They're not ready for a serious commitment. Much like a cheating spouse in a long-term relationship; they're not looking to leave but they're looking for that feel good factor that is missing where they are

right now.

4. You put them off and they didn't know how to say it. If you stop trying to "close" them and instead give them the option to do more research before making a commitment this shouldn't happen. That being said, even if you follow the plan some people do just change their mind, calm down, or have their partners talk them out of it. They're human beings remember–they're volatile by nature!

5. You did the dirty and telephone interviewed them. Possibly with the worst person and not the best person. Double whammy. On the call they may have agreed to meet but the experience was so one sided and horrible that they were never going to attend – they just didn't have the guts to give you the feedback there and then.

To keep candidates engaged in the process, to effectively "put a ring on it", you have to make them feel good and keep them wanting more but only after you have decided they're worth it.

Here's what the ultimate candidate process should look like:

ABC formula to assess

Confirm for interview or reject nicely

Confirm interview with same day confirmation

Share quality information and prep

Trigger email sequence

On day reminder message and text

There is of course post-interview engagement but we'll talk about that in the next chapter. For now we just want to make sure that once you have got a good person into your pipeline they stay there.

This means you filter and assess in a way that feels good to them. If you do confirm a meeting you confirm formally the same day and you make sure you share the right type of content to prepare them AND excite them.

You should then be triggering an automated sequence of emails reminding them of your meeting but also sharing a unique fact, video or insight in each one to assert the many reasons why it would be great for them to work for your company – you must keep reminding them of this to keep their interest and excitement at optimum levels and keep them motivated to attend. The cooling off period is dangerous.

I'll share a little story on how I got to this system...

When I first started out on my journey into the world of Rec2Rec I was baffled. I had grossly underestimated how much business was out there and how many companies needed this new breed of service we offered but I had equally grossly overestimated how candidates would behave.

I had spent years looking at Rec2Rec agencies and scoffing at their shoddy service, their lack of investment, their clear lack of technical knowledge. It seemed little more than lifting CVs from CV boards and spraying them out by email hoping for a hit.

But the reality I faced in year one of launching Recruiter Republic was a hard one. I have to admit my ego didn't like it one little bit. I had worked my way up to Director at Hays; I had a large region with lots of employees and managed massive budgets. And here I was being giving the run around by Recruitment Consultants with six months experience.

Of course it's easier to see things clearly with a little time and distance but at the time I know that I allowed my ego get in the way a little. I dismissed what I saw as flaky behaviour and effectively shut off the candidate but I realised, over time, that while some candidates absolutely should be cut loose, I had to accept that some good candidates were also falling off the hook. Some good candidates, despite what they said, had behaviour that was contrary to their words. Whether I liked the fact that a junior Consultant didn't respect me or not I had to let that go.

When I allowed my inner geek to explore the problem I started to see patterns. And after refining, testing and re-trialling I discovered a process that worked. Since then I have helped numerous companies improve their attracting and interview strategies. During that time certain patterns emerged:

1. The conversion ratio of interviews actually confirmed to interviews completed DOUBLED when the interview confirmation was sent formally via email and on the same day.

2. The interviews with a follow up sequence leading up to the interview date also enjoyed an enhanced conversion ratio, but another interesting upside was that post-interview feedback was stronger on both sides. I think this was largely because they were already warmed up to the client, that anything shared in the build-up made them feel safer, more informed and more confident.

As soon as you accept that Recruiters aren't flaky but they are time poor, that they are cynical and fearful and also stressed a lot of the time, you will have more empathy for them. If you assess them properly and give them an organised framework to make it easy to stay committed to the plan, the good guys stay in process.

CHAPTER 10

INTERVIEW FUNNEL – PIMP YOUR PROCESS

I haven't sat in on an interview with you before, but I am pretty sure there are probably some key areas of the interview you typically conduct that could be drastically improved.

If you're anything like most recruitment leaders I know, then you probably fall into the trap of interviewing off-the-cuff. It's largely a gut instinct led process and no two interviews follow the same format.

Maybe you've never been given the secret formula before, maybe you're so busy you don't have time to prepare for interviews so you're winging it a lot of the time, maybe you're just old school and you just eyeball your candidate and it flows from there. Perhaps, you have a very templated structure but it's not that engaging for the candidate.

The list is long when it comes to the reasons why so many interviews create a negative impression for your ideal candidates – but after a lot of time and money researching this, interviewing candidates and monitoring (we've even filmed for a lot of companies to show them), we can pretty much see the same issues that crop up time and time again.

Here are the top 10 interview fails in the eyes of the candidate:

- No preparation by you for the interview

- No email confirmation or instructions for the meeting

- Accessing building / reception is complicated

- Kept waiting in reception

- Interview starts late

- Interview palmed off to someone else without warning and only find out on the day

- Interviewed by someone more junior than them or HR/IR

- Interview interrupted by person or phone

- Interview style aggressive

- Interviewer antagonistic

- Interviewer has not read CV in advance

This research allowed me to design and test a much stronger interview process for our clients; one that eliminates the turn offs for the candidates and amplifies their interest while still allowing for thorough assessment.

Every single company that I have shared this process with has said that it is EASIER to do and converts MORE candidates to the next stage. So take it from me – this works.

It starts with the end in mind. Your ideal goal is to ensure that the person you offer joins. Which means that their experience in interview has to be GREAT.

From how you communicate with them before interview and how you prepare prior to the interview, through to the way they are greeted, the room they are interviewed in, the people they meet and the interview process itself; it all adds up to the impression your candidate takes away.

It's how they FEEL as a result of the interview that dictates whether they want to join your team or not. And whether you like it or not, candidates are human beings and they are dominated by emotion rather than logical thinking. So no matter how logical a conclusion you think it would be to want to accept an offer with you, if you did not make them FEEL great they won't convert.

You know this. You've seen a great candidate reject your offer and accept one with a firm you would deem far less progressive than yours. They accept an offer that isn't as strong, on a less exciting desk and with less inspirational people. So why?

Because of how they were made to feel during the interview process.

They made their decision based on their emotions rather than logic. Emotions win every time. So you need a way to really assess your candidate to ensure they are right for your business but all the while make them feel GREAT about the opportunity to join.

And this is where most people get the interview process wrong. They wait to make someone feel good until AFTER they decide they are a potential good fit good – by then it's often too late. The candidate has been turned off.

Or some people SELL, SELL, SELL, to the candidate in interview but never get a real reading on who they are and if they are right for their team.

So let's start with what we want to happen, then review that against what currently happens so that you can identify the areas that will dramatically improve your process..

THE AIM OF THE INTERVIEW

Let's keep this simple. The interview is there to understand if the candidate is right for you and for you to make them want to join your firm.

So your interview process should assess their experience, personality, goals and ambitions to ensure they are the right candidate for you. All the while you are making them feel GREAT about working for you.

YOUR INTERVIEW FORMULA

Build a bond + find pain + show empathy + agitate pain + offer solution + brand new day + proof

Scenario based interviewing

Remember we talked about this earlier? This formula sits behind your marketing, telephone calls and goes into full swing in the face-to-face interview.

This is your overarching formula for the interview too. The top line is the candidate experience the bottom line is your assessment.

Before we can structure the interview and give you a template you first need to create hero quality scenarios and understand scenario based interviewing.

SO WHAT IS A SCENARIO-BASED INTERVIEW?

Well for those of you that understand competency based interviews this will be pretty easy to adopt but for those of you that don't here is a crash course.

Competency based interviewing is where you ask specific interview questions designed to uncover a candidate's qualities and experience. It's designed to rid the interview of fluffy or expected interview answers and instead seek real life experiences that demonstrate the specific candidate qualities you seek.

So for example, if you are looking for loyalty as a quality in a normal competency based interview you would ask something like "tell me about a time where you had to demonstrate your loyalty in a testing situation". Now as a competency based interview, it's definitely a better question than asking someone straight up if they are loyal (because it's obvious what the answer should be), but it's still not that hard to anticipate what the interviewer wants to hear in this situation.

A scenario-based question is a little different. It starts off as a hypothetical question so that you can work through the course of action your candidate would take in that scenario and can then be further supported by asking the question again by making relevant to something that has already happened.

Let me use the same theme of loyalty for ease

Q1: "Can you imagine being in a scenario where your Manager seems to be grumpy all the time and over-critical. It's starting to make you feel miserable and one day your Director notices and calls you in for a chat. Your Manager has been good to you in the past, they haven't always been this way, you have a feeling it's temporary and that some-thing is happening in their personal life so you're definitely feeling conflicted. What would you do? Do you share your thoughts with your Director? Do you keep them to yourself or do you try something else?

Q2: Whatever the answer follow-up with probing questions to understand their rationale. "Why do you think that is the right course of action? What other options do you have?". "What are the possible outcomes?"

Once you are satisfied that you have understood their answers fully you can then take it back to a competency based interview question.

For example:

"Can you tell me about a specific time where felt your loyalty was really tested?"

The candidate will invariably give you an abridged answer – it will be up to you to ask probing questions using the **STAR** technique to be able to assess their answers full.

Situation – the detail surrounding the scenario to set the scene

Task – what was needed and why

Action – the specific steps they took to achieve their goal

Results – the specific output they achieved AND what they learned

You also follow up with what the candidate has learned since then and what they would do differently if they could.

You are getting real insight into how they have behaved in the past as well as how they would now behave in the future based on what they have learned.

Threaded through all this of course has to be a charismatic approach to the conversation.

So let's map out some scenario based questions based on the hero qualities you seek. You will have five to seven hero qualities that you seek and for each quality you can probably think of two to three scenarios at least that would demonstrate that quality. So if you put some time into this you can create a library of these that you rotate.

Here's an example for you:

HERO QUALITY	SCENARIO QUESTION	EVIDENCE SOUGHT	YOUR ASSESSMENT
Ability to work independently without constant input	If you had a hot vacancy registered, what would your first 5 activities be and why?	Job control (TOB agreed , visit arranged, full spec agreed, candidate criteria agreed, activity so far uncovered, timescales agreed) + Prioritisation (is it workable over other jobs) + Immediate job filling tasks (database search, colleague referrals, advert, headhunts, mailshot)	Good job control ideas but missed agreeing a timescale. Good job filling tasks but didn't use colleague referrals. Came up with a good idea re asking client who was a no. **Score – 8/10**

We will come back to these shortly to know when to use them.

Here is your interview structure broken down to show you how the formula applies to your overall approach, the progress of covering CV and history while finding the right time to use scenario based interview questions.

ELEMENT	BOND	PAIN	EMPATHY	MORE PAIN
Approach	Meet & Greet Matching & Mirroring Friendly & open	Probing questions Lots of notes How do issues make them feel?	Probe around how their issues make them feel and show empathy	How will that feel? What impact will this have?
Content	Set the agenda for what you want to cover, who they might meet	Ask them to recap career so far and why they might be open to a move	Share your personal stories – don't have to be the same issue but the same feeling	Encourage them to anticipate how they will feel in 12 months if their problems still remain
SBIQ	Identify a scenario linked to a pain point and use STAR technique			Scenario 2– future scenario
Scoring	/ 10	/ 10	/ 10	/ 10

SOLUTIONS	NEW DAY	PROOF	NEXT STEPS	FEEDBACK
If they could access these things how would that impact their performance and happiness? How would they feel?	Painting a detailed picture of life for them at your firm	Social proof of what is possible	Guage their interest in progressing	Give them specifics about what you like about them and why they would be a good fit for your team
Outline the unique qualities, tools, systems or features they will access if they join	Talk in assumptive language about where they will be, and how they will feel when they join	Give them proof of the change that is possible by sharing a real case study of someone in your team today	If you know you like them tell them there and then that you absolutely want them to come back	Ask them to share their feedback as to what they are attracted to, what their reservations are
	Scenario 3–based on their own identified key challenge		SBIQ Score	
				/15
/ 10	/ 10	/ 10	Y / N	Note concerns

You will see I have also added on next steps and feedback. This is a major part of the process that MUST be communicated directly to the candidate while they are with you. It's also very important for you to assess their level of interest while they are with you.

You should be scoring as you go. For how well they work to build rapport with you, how well they tell their story about their experiences to date and the reasons for them exploring new options. Also how they feel about their current situation and what they now seek elsewhere.

How they respond to your scenario based questions will be very important – so you need to score as you go. A great tip here is NOT to use seven. Ever. It forces you not to sit on the fence.

THE IMPORTANCE OF FEEDBACK

We are in a market where there are more roles than there are experienced candidates we cannot play this "you first" game; it makes no sense! I know why you do it. I used to do it too.

It went a little something like this…

I bring someone in for interview.

They are better in person that I expected them to be.

After grilling them a bit, I start to wake up and try to sell them the role back a little.

I get them biting back that they want the job.

I discover the have other interviews with competitors yet to happen.

I then push them away to test if they really want it and will fight for the job after they have seen the others.

I lose them to a competitor who made them feel good, even though I know their company, rewards, training, role, desk and wider team is nowhere near the same standard at all.

They made them feel good – I didn't.

Ridiculous right? Do you recognise it though?

I know why you probably do it. You're trying to scare them off now rather than later. You want them to judge your firm more highly than the others. After all, they should be able to see the difference shouldn't they?

In your eyes, pushing them away now if their reasons are weak will save you a lot of time, cash and frustration later.

But please remember that with your new approach you will have far more heroes in process, and if you follow the interview plan you will still be filtering and assessing. But from the start you make them feel good – that is the only difference.

PRE INTERVIEW CHECKLIST

Before you go and implement your new interview template it's worth completing another exercise to understand the candidate experience.

Go do a walk through. Go to your building entrance and try and take everything in with fresh eyes – you do it all the time so you can't see it clearly. Ask yourself these questions:

- Is your office easy to find based on the information sent out?

- What's the first impression of your building and reception?

- How are you greeted?

- What is the reception/waiting area like?

- What is the interview room like?

The reason I ask you to do this is that first impressions count. The human brain forms an opinion on an environment or new person within seconds. Before they even meet you they have pre-framed the interview based on how they "feel" when they first meet your company. You need to ensure this experience is good. Do you know how many firms don't brief their interviewees about a strange set up in reception? Or don't greet their candidates personally or don't have a good process for announcing their arrival? Or don't know where the candidate is placed to wait for them?

It all frames your interview in negative light. So go do a review and make any changes you need to. If you can, you should have a specific interview room set aside for this purpose that is kept pristine and has good quality information on the walls (think awards, news, stories, accolades and more).

So all pretty easy stuff to fix, right?

You now know how to identify your hero, how to structure your interview and how to use scenario based interview questions to understand and assess their suitability. You're engaging them and making sure they get good immediate feedback AND a great first impression when they come to meet you.

Let me challenge you in one area of your process that you probably need to rethink...

WHO CONDUCTS YOUR FIRST INTERVIEWS?

By far, the absolute number one pet hate that experienced Recruiters rant about is being interviewed by internal recruiters, or perhaps worse, people they would consider peers or juniors.

It makes them feel dismissed, unimportant and like they're being screened for the big boss...and we both know they're probably right.

So how do know if you have the right person in place?

Here's a quick way to tell...

Who would you send to a major client meeting that could win you £1M of fee revenue over the next few years? That's the person that does the interviews; it might be you and it might be one of your Directors or Managers. But you need to know they are GREAT in interview.

You absolutely cannot put someone weak on the front line and only allow good people to meet you or your best people if they pass the first meeting. Guess what? The good ones don't want to come back.

We've already accepted that attracting and converting great people is the number one priority for your business. You absolutely must put your best people in charge of meeting people. Anyone that you have involved in the interview process that wouldn't cut the mustard with a major client pitch should be taken out of the process immediately.

Don't say you're busy or you don't have enough time. This is your business and the issue of talent is your number one issue. Make time. You're not going to waste time on poor interviews if you adopt this system. This is your first priority above and beyond anything else and you have to put the absolute best person on this. If that's you so be it.

Let your juniors, HR or IR people do Graduate / Trainee interviews where it's not quite so important. But for experienced hires, instant fee generating Recruiters that can add £200K per year to your fee line...they get the VIP treatment every time.

CHAPTER 11

"THE PROPOSAL" A.K.A. YOUR OFFER PROCESS

You've done it! You've found someone you really like and they seem to like your company too. But it's way too early to pat yourself on the back just yet.

Your work is far from over.

This stage of the process can be heartbreaking for some people that have worked hard to find someone they like only to lose them at offer stage. And I'm not talking about counter offers – we'll cover that in the next chapter.

I'm talking about losing them before they even verbally accept an offer.

So let's start with why. We've researched this one endlessly and here are the REAL reasons why candidates disconnect at offer stage.

- Lowball offer. Either lower than industry, lower than stated earlier in the process or lower than originally suggested.

- Offer took too long to come out in writing

- New employer insisted on acceptance without releasing contract, handbook or other key info

- Offer wasn't delivered in person and key data was misunderstood (Particularly commission)

- Offer made too bullishly as "take it or leave it"

- New employer took references without permission and before candidate had resigned

- Employer asked for proof of billings too late in the process

- Final interview process too brutal and scared them off

The crazy thing about pretty much all of these is that they are all avoidable and cost nothing to fix! It's all just process, strategy or planning.

Let's look at each one so you can take action and make sure it doesn't block your next superstar.

LOWBALL OFFER

Now I call this "lowball" as of course this is the candidate perspective. So how does this happen? Well usually it's because you either haven't established the candidate's expectation so you're just in different places in terms of expectation or you know what they expect but you haven't communicated or discussed what an offer would look like and assessed their response. It's very rare that a candidate will accept an offer after feeling the initial deflation of a lowball offer. Even if you later increase it they can't forget how they felt. So two quick win action points for you.

1. Establish early what their expectation is on salary and package. But I have to warn you on this; there is a difference between what someone is worth in the market generally and what they are worth to you; and both have little link to what they are currently paid. There is a strange fascination about proving current salaries that kills candidates in process. Just pay someone what they are worth to you with guidance from them in terms of their expectation. Don't fall into the bear trap of just offering a slight improvement to someone's current salary or package as unfortunately this nearly always loses you the candidate.

2. Before you make the offer you should be discussing it in detail with them to understand what will come next and to guage their reaction. If there's an issue face it head on and talk it through. Then it can't be seen as a "lowball" and you can make sure you influence the outcome.

THE OFFER TAKES TOO LONG TO COME OUT IN WRITING

Have you ever put an offer on a house? Or waited for a test result? Do you remember how time suddenly moves so much more slowly when you're waiting to hear about an important life decision where you can't control the outcome? It's very easy for anticipation and excitement to turn into something far more negative. And the longer the time lapse the more likely your candidate is to be receptive to an alternative offer. An offer from someone who might well make them feel more important.

1. Take a look at your current process for issuing offers and understand what prevents an offer from going out the same day it is made verbally.

2. **Do you have a template offer document pack already?** If not get that done.

3. **Is it perhaps your offer approval or sign-off process that causes an issue?** If so, then perhaps implement an online document signing solution – not only will it enable you to store templates and adapt easily but you can send to be signed by anyone that needs to authorise before sending out.

4. Your potential new team member doesn't care if you are busy or if you have a lot on or if HR haven't got round to sorting it out yet. And nor should they. If you have a delay here; fix it.

INSUFFICIENT INFORMATION

It is so frustrating for a candidate to await an offer in writing – only to receive a pretty flimsy email or basic letter. When a candidate awaits an offer in writing they want everything. Their contract, their full offer letter and conditions, and a full breakdown of your commission and employee scheme; and on this point, don't assume your commission scheme is easy to understand. You may well have a huge advantage to the way your scheme works compared to their current model. So work it through with them and be transparent with real worked examples.

Either way, whatever you do, don't get caught up in making too brief an offer and then expecting a response that is meaningful. This is how many firms believe they have an offer accepted when they don't. Again if you have everything set up as a template and it includes all of the above information you eliminate this as a problem.

OFFER WASN'T DELIVERED IN PERSON

This is a subtle issue and it isn't necessarily one that a candidate will complain about however we know from our research that offers just sent on an email have a far lower acceptance rate than those discussed in person and presented face to face. Now it may well be that you need to release the offer to keep the candidate engaged but in my experience if you can, an offer delivered in person has far greater impact, allows the candidate to ask questions instead of drawing incorrect conclusions and allows you the opportunity to close them and seal the deal. The more formal it feels to the candidate the less likely they are to fall out of the process later.

OFFER MADE TOO BULLISHLY AS "TAKE IT OR LEAVE IT"

Imagine you're looking for a new role because you feel a little unloved and undervalued where you are now. And imagine finding a firm you like but just as you get excited about a potential offer it is issued in a take it or leave it manner. Like you're disposable. Like the firm is more important than you. Like you're nothing special. How would that make you feel? Does it make you feel wanted and valued? If the reason for adopting a "take it or leave it" stance in the first place is an attempt to avoid a bidding war then I understand, but this isn't the way to do it. All it will do is push away your candidate.

When you make an offer it should be delivered in a positive and enthusiastic way and should clearly communicate to the candidate why you want them to join, the scope of the opportunity and how you see them succeeding over the short, medium and long term.

Just the fact that you're willing to sit down and talk through what the future holds for them, how their bonuses and commission will work and how they will be supported will be seen as so valuable and representative of working with you that few will be able to resist. While others will just send an email your approach will make them feel far more special.

NEW EMPLOYER TOOK REFERENCES WITHOUT PERMISSION AND BEFORE CANDIDATE HAD RESIGNED

It constantly amazes me, in a market so short on talent, why anyone would go and start asking questions about someone without their permission and potentially offend them or worse cause them a serious issue with their current employer.

How would you feel if you after making a verbal offer the candidate called your ex employer to find out why you left and what you're like? Or called your ex-employees to find out why they left?

If you're not sure about someone spend more time with them or ask for reference information. But it comes after the offer and with permission. Anywhere else is totally inappropriate; not only does it leave you wide open for legal action but more importantly you will nearly always lose the candidate anyway so what's the point? But by far the worst damage to your brand is that other potential recruits will find out about it and it stops other people ever stepping forward.

EMPLOYER ASKED FOR PROOF OF BILLINGS TOO LATE IN THE PROCESS

If gaining proof of billings is a requirement, tell people early in the process rather than further down the line that it will be required to facilitate an offer. Why? Because many Recruiters fall into the trap of overstating their salary, commission or fees in order to negotiate a better deal. If you wait until the point of offer to suddenly ask for proof of billings you will increase the risk of losing them. And the only reason for it will be that they have been caught in a compromising position. You probably would have offered them anyway. So let them know early then it's not a surprise and your candidate is far likelier to be honest about their rewards and results.

FINAL INTERVIEW PROCESS TOO BRUTAL AND SCARED THEM OFF

So you really like someone and you get them back for a final interview. But then decide to really put them through their paces. Make them prove how much they want it. Really flush out any issues. And there's nothing like terrorising your candidate is there for finding out what they're really made of is there?

What? This just can't happen. But it does. A lot.

Do you know how jarring this is to the candidate? To be invited back, excited about their prospects, hoping that an offer might be made only to find that the person interviewing them doesn't believe their reasons for moving, doesn't believe their achievements on their CV and even criticises their other interview choices.

What a complete turn off.

What's even more bizarre is quite often once you have managed to scare them off you tell yourself it's a good thing as clearly they didn't want it enough or they weren't made of the right stuff.

The final interview can of course be a final assessment of the candidate's suitability but you still use the same formula. Your candidate should still feel good about it.

You wouldn't accept this behaviour the other way around – even though it is a candidate led market.

Can you imagine?

A candidate coming back for a final and quizzing you over your company figures in a cynical manner? Can you visualise a candidate questioning your reasons for recruiting someone as maybe not being about expansion and more about a retention issue? Can you imagine a candidate quizzing you about who else you have interviewed and then questioning your intelligence for even considering them?

And wait – can you imagine them saying they're not even interested in talking about and offer unless you confirm you're rejecting everyone else and won't be seeing any of them for further interviews?

Honestly there is no way you would accept it. So don't do it.

CHAPTER 12

"IT'S NOT ME, IT'S YOU" – RESIGNATION & ACCEPTANCE FUNNEL

We've come a long way. We've completely rewritten your process.

We've identified your ideal candidate and crafted your employer value proposition around it.

We've seen how to maximise your traffic routes to drive people to your careers page.

We've automated a nurture marketing campaign to maximise the 40% of the market not just 4%.

We've engaged people in a way that makes them feel good but still assesses them thoroughly for fit.

We've given them a great interview experience and made an offer in the right way.

All good, yes?

Nearly…

So, you've got an offer accepted. But your work is not yet complete. Sorry – but we're nearly there I promise.

We all know that any candidate worth their salt will hit a company hard when they leave – we did the sums earlier about the financial impact of a resignation. And no Boss likes to be fired by an employee. One resignation, as you know, is enough to derail your entire business plan for the year so it's no wonder that pretty much every experienced Recruiter finds themselves at the receiving end of a counter offer when they resign.

On that basis, if this new hire is important to you, you must manage it. Many new employers ignore this stage of the process at their peril, incorrectly assuming that it has nothing to do with them. Wrong.

So where do you get involved? How do you protect your new hire? Well we both know that any candidate is capable of changing their mind. They are human beings after all. And some candidates are more likely than others to accept a counter – listen out for the reasons for looking for a new role.

The candidates that feel undervalued are often the most likely to fall for a counter. The attention and respect they feel they aren't given and actually crave comes washing over them at resignation stage.

That attention they have craved for so long is now theirs in abundance and it's horribly seductive. Much like the profuse apologies of an abusive partner once their victim threatens to leave.

It's temporary, it won't change anything and it's a measure of control while a new plan is put into place. You and I can see it – but they can't.

Your best plan in all cases is to assume that

1. There will be a counter; and

2. They are open to one

3. They won't always tell you how they really feel about it.

While you can't completely control what will happen, you can manage this process, stay ahead of the loop and minimise your chances of losing someone to a counter.

And if you do lose them to a counter you can ensure the door is open for them to come back to you when they come to their senses – and at least half the time they will.

Here's your process for managing the acceptance and resignation process but don't forget; identifying their motives during the interview process and playing devil's advocate usually identifies those most likely to be swayed by a counter.

OFFER ACCEPTANCE

Make an offer acceptance formal and wherever possible in person. There are two reasons for this;

1. It makes it more real and formal to your candidate

2. If they are unsure they will tend to delay or avoid this which is an early flag

RESIGNATION

Confirm upon offer acceptance the date your candidate plans to resign. Coach them through what to expect and how to expect a counter. Make sure they know that anyone that resigns has a big financial impact on a company and that all counters are designed to simply slow the situation down and make alternative plans. Remind them of why they wanted to leave and why they have accepted. Offer them some support in recognition that resigning can be quite a tough thing to do.

Arrange to meet them that day for lunch or straight after work for a drink. You need to stay involved and supportive. Again if they avoid this it's a red flag and it's better to know early rather than late.

START DATE & SOCIAL

Once you know resignation has been accepted confirm the start date of your new employee and arrange a midpoint date for team drinks, meal or social. You need to break up the notice period, and mentally move them in. Meeting the team in a social environment will be a great pre-start bonding experience also. So win-win all round.

CATCH UPS

You should schedule two further calls or coffee meetings around the social date if possible. You can use a variety of reasons – set up of preferences for IT, mobile phone hand over, set up for payroll. Find a reason to have a conversation that ties in to their start and use it as an opportunity to stay connected, ask them how they're feeling and listen for clues. If you sense something isn't right then probe. If they're all set to start then you are simply engaging and caring about getting them off to a good start.

PRE-START ENGAGEMENT

If you're really smart you will use your email nurture sequence to pre-onboard your new team member with a series of emails designed to get them excited about their imminent start, introduce them to key people online, show them key benefits and generally retain the excitement level they felt at offer acceptance. It should be a stark contrast to what they are experiencing if they're still in their old role post resignation.

And if you're super smart you'll get a referral campaign in here also. Don't ask before resignation it's too early, but after…go for it. Throughout this stage remember one thing:

IF THE FEELING IS MUTUAL THE EFFORT WILL BE EQUAL.

If your new hire's behaviour indicates otherwise it does not mean you should withdraw your offer. It means you pay attention and treat it as a caution rather than simply wait until their start date.

CHAPTER 13

"ALL ABOARD" – OTHERWISE KNOWN AS ONBOARDING

Remember what we talked about at the start in our myth busting chapters? You know...that crazy myth that experienced Recruiters don't adapt well and then leave??

Well your onboarding process is a major part of ensuring your new recruit is happy AND productive in those early days and weeks. Once again, these steps are FREE so no budget implications here but they do require some advance thinking and organisation. But if you imple-ment them do they have a BIG impact.

Let's remind ourselves of what you want out of this.

You want a happy new starter that's productive quickly and sticks around...yes?

Well then, we want your new starter to be welcomed, to have a clear expectation of what you need them to do and basic housekeeping done so that all of that experience you are paying for is put to good use and is not wasted on clearing out drawers, trying to make their mouse work or trying to figure out the detail of their desk (just some of the ridiculous things recruiters find themselves doing on their first day).

So instead of manically dashing around the night before they are due to start, emptying their desk and trying to generate log-ins let's do this properly. Let's make them feel like you're taking this seriously – because you know what? If you do they will too.

Your preparation checklist should include:

- Induction

- Team Preparation

- Systems Set up

- Desk Preparation

- Week one–four project plan

- Buddy system

- Four week review date set

Let's break them down to make sure you have the right content (I've got some great templates you can use – details at the end).

INDUCTION

Your induction should cover the usual basics in terms of H&S, HR, Payroll, Who's Who and all the usual fun stuff. Don't underestimate what needs to be included and talked through here; especially things like building access, hours of work, what to do if absent from work or in an emergency, where to get lunch or drinks etc. These things put people at ease.

TEAM PREPARATION

If you don't have one already create a floor plan of who sits where, what they do and their extension numbers and emails. The quicker someone feels part of things and can do simple things like confidently pass on messages or answer calls, the better. A really good icebreaker is to get someone that is well liked and friendly to introduce them to each team.

SYSTEMS

Do you know how many new recruits aren't shown how their tele-phone works? The very thing you want them to use the most and want to see them use quickly!! So phones, PC, mobiles and either explainer videos, or light touch intros are needed for all your key IT platforms. If you have access control, office keys or alarm systems that would affect your new starter make sure you cover this off too.

DESK PREPARATION

This is the one that makes a big impact on how quickly your new starter will be productive. So you may need to get an administrator or resourcer on the case here but it will totally be worth it. Work through to clean, update and compile the following information:

- Breakdown of live, lapsed and prospect clients – segmented

- Cleansed list of live vacancies and all notes on your CRM

- 5 fresh candidate leads – candidates that have been screened or generated

- Book five client meetings with a colleague or Manager

- Print off TOB

- Candidate hot lists / searches

- An outline email campaign for current roles ready to go

- An intro email introducing your new starter to your clients ready to go

- Summary of desk history and opportunities

- Doing this makes your new team member feel like you're making an effort for them. For you, it means there is nowhere to hide; your new Consultant has valuable activities to get stuck into quickly.

WEEK ONE – FOUR WEEK PROJECT PLAN

If a new placement is going to fail it's because expectations have not been set, communicated and agreed either way. Setting a project for completion for the first four weeks sets those expectations early, allows your new team member to work with some independence and gives them the opportunity to communicate what they need in order to deliver. If you know what they need and they know what you need you are far more likely to get it. You can then replicate for weeks 5 - 12.

PART THREE

CHAPTER 14

THE WAY TO GET STARTED IS TO QUIT TALKING AND BEGIN DOING

I don't know about you but once I have a plan I need to get started before everyday life takes over. There's something infectious about taking an immediate step towards your goal and making progress with your plan of attack. One step invariably leads to another. But it all starts with getting started. From experience this is where most people fail. Despite having the will, the resources, and the plan they fail because they don't take action.

So instead of becoming overwhelmed by the long to do list you may be creating in your mind the best approach is to take this one chunk at a time. Please don't fall into the trap of parking this...because I guarantee, before you know it you're back to doing what you've always done and nothing will fundamentally change.

Part Three is simply a checklist, a play by play set of steps for you to now take and put all of this into action.

I have no idea as to how much or how little help you might need to get this done. Some of this might simply be a jolt to your perspective and will simply be an energizer to go away and improve the framework you already have, maybe what you have is already pretty good but just one or two takeaways from what I have shared will be enough to transform your talent pipeline, maybe for you this is a complete system build (and in some cases this is the best because you get to build it right first time but on the downside this can also be the most daunting).

Either way I want to make sure you have everything you need to help you to get started and get doing. To help you, I have created a page-by-page set of activities to take you through EVERYTHING you need to do to implement each of these steps.

In addition I have created a host of further templates, downloads, help videos and deep dive coaching sessions for those of you that want to take this to the next level as well as **One Day Intensive Workshops** – where you come and work with me and a handful of peers with similar challenges (but not competitors) to get this done together. Whatever your preferred method of putting this into action, there is a solution and help available.

All your extra resources can be found here:

www.rec2recsecrets.com/book/downloads

Take each stage in isolation and complete. They bolt together at the end.

Take it one stage at a time.

Remember – change by the inch is a cinch. Change by the yard is hard.

STEP ONE: HEROES, VILLAINS & CANDIDATE MINDSET

THE TALENT FORMULA

**Build a bond + find pain + show empathy + agitate pain
+ offer solution + brand new day + proof**

SCENARIO BASED INTERVIEWING

Notes

Preparation at this stage acts as the bedrock for what comes next. To create compelling adverts, career pages, emails, interview plans and social content you must define who you are trying to attract and why they should be attracted to your company while also repelling your villain. Spending time now to think this through and matching your hero's pain to your solutions while building a vision for their "brand new day" with you, will result in a fluid and strong core messaging that you will keep coming back to. Time invested here will always be well spent.

TO DO LIST

- Create the key characteristics, advantages and features of joining your team

- Create your Hero Profile and their typical pain

- Create your Villain Profile and their typical pain

- Create your empathy stories based on expected hero pain

- Create a list of "solutions" your team / company can offer in answer to those pain points

- Create a "brand new day profile"

- Create case studies (two-five) of people that have joined and transformed in a similar way

Tools

For free template downloads and further online resources visit:

www.rec2recsecrets.com/book/downloads

STEP TWO: YOUR TALENT ATTRACTION FUNNEL

SETTING UP YOUR ATTRACTION CHANNELS

CAREER PAGES

Notes

Before you create content you need the right infrastructure. That means creating the right channels and generating some base content on each BEFORE you start building out your networks aggressively. I have listed the key channels I would recommend but if you know your markets will benefit from using Snapchat or Pinterest then go for it. As a starting point get them created, tailor them to suit your company employer brand visually and ensure you have all the right key contact information listed.

TO DO LIST

- Create a life@companyname Instagram account

- Create a careers@companyname showcase page on Linkedin

- Create a careers@companyname Facebook account

- Create a careers@companyname Twitter account

- Create a company careers page

Tools

For ideas, tutorials and additional coaching modules on how to easily create compelling content for these channels (including templates you can clone) visit this page:

www.rec2recsecrets.com/book/downloads

STEP THREE: YOUR ASSESSMENT PROCESS

It's as easy as ABC

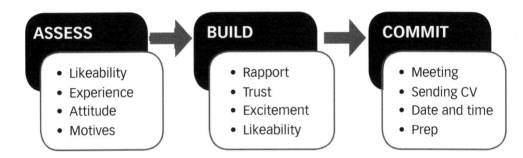

ASSESS
- Likeability
- Experience
- Attitude
- Motives

BUILD
- Rapport
- Trust
- Excitement
- Likeability

COMMIT
- Meeting
- Sending CV
- Date and time
- Prep

Notes

Assessing your candidates initially on the telephone should not feel like a telephone interview; it is designed to ASSESS their personality and experience at a high level and if that matches what you look for, then you spend time to BUILD their trust in you and your company. You deepen their attraction by highlighting what joining your team might look like and once you have done this you see COMMITMENT to a face to face interview. You should have a template for this so that anyone taking these calls conducts this in the same way.

TO DO LIST

- Create an assessment template for telephone calls / enquiries with new candidates

- Lay out the criteria you seek in a candidate to be of interest based on experience, reasons for a move, pain, personality and phone manner

- Layout a few steps for building their trust and attraction

- Layout an agreed process for arranging an interview and gain commitment there and then

- Have a process for saving assessment sheet to refer back to before interview

- Create email template for confirming interviews

- Create email nurture sequence for candidates on interview

Tools

For a free template download that can edit and amend to suit you or for further videos and guides to help you assess candidates visit this page:

www.rec2recsecrets.com/book/downloads

STEP FOUR : YOUR TALENT ATTRACTION PROCESS

Your Interview Funnel

ELEMENT	BOND	PAIN	EMPATHY	MORE PAIN
Approach	Meet & Greet Matching & Mirroring Friendly & open	Probing questions Lots of notes How do issues make them feel?	Probe around how their issues make them feel?	How will that feel? What impact will this have?
Content	Set the agenda for what you want to cover, who they might meet	Ask them to recap career so far and why they might be open to a move	Share your personal stories – don't have to be the same issue but the same feeling	Encourage them to anticipate how they will feel if 12 months from now they are still in the same role with issues remaining
SBIQ		Identify a scenario linked to a pain point and use STAR technique		
Scoring	/ 10	/ 10	/ 10	/ 10

SOLUTIONS	NEW DAY	PROOF	NEXT STEPS	FEEDBACK
If they could access these things how would that impact their performance and happiness? How would they feel?	Painting a detailed picture of life for them at your firm	Social proof of what is possible	Gauge their interest in progressing	Give them specifics about what you like about them and why they would be a good fit for your team
Outline the unique qualities, tools, systems or features they will access if they join	Talk in assumptive language about where they will be, what desk they could have and what their opportunity would be	Give them proof of the change that is possible by sharing a real case study of someone in your team today	If you know you like them tell them there and then that you absolutely want them to come back and spend more time exploring the opportunity	Ask them to share their feedback as to what they are attracted to, what their reservations are
Scenario 2– future scenario	Scenario 3– based on their own identified key challenge	Scenario 4– based on a challenge you think they will have		
/ 10	/ 10	/ 10	N / A	

Notes:

Remember only your best people should be interviewing potential candidates and you should all be working to the same framework of the talent formula. This should be something that is trained into your team – if you need help with this then use the link at the bottom for more resources. What's important is that you have a process and a universal scoring system and interview template.

TO DO LIST

- Review and improve your candidate experience from arrival at building to end of interview

- Decide who your best people are to interview and restrict it to only them

- Create your team interview template and scoresheet

- Book a coaching session with that team on how to manage the interview

- Create a universally agreed system to uploading notes and triggering next stage process

- Create your interview engagement email sequence

Tools

For FREE templates and further videos and coaching resources to help your team to interview in a way that really converts or how to map out and manage an automated email sequence visit this page:

www.rec2recsecrets.com/book/downloads

STEP FIVE: YOUR OFFER PROCESS

Proposal V Ultimatum

Notes

Remember offers should be made immediately and presented in person wherever possible. Time drags at this stage of the process increase your chances of losing someone so automate the parts that you can (such as raising the actual offer). Remind yourself of the bad habits to avoid and remove from your process immediately.

TO DO LIST

- Create offer document template including commission, benefits, contract etc.

- Review sign-off process and improve with online document signature if needed.

- Coach anyone involved in making offers on your agreed process.

- Coach OUT any bad habits.

- Coach your key people on how to present an offer in person and in a way that feels. GOOD and is not an ultimatum.

Tools

For free templates and additional guidance and training videos on how to manage the offer process visit:

www.rec2recsecrets.com/book/downloads

STEP SIX: YOUR INTERVIEW PROCESS
– ACCEPTANCE & RESIGNATION

Notes

The acceptance and resignation process costs nothing to manage and doubles your acceptance rate when managed properly. It's a very straightforward process to automate. It starts with making acceptance formal and should then trigger a sequence of events that can be automated including email sequences to keep your new team member engaged and excited about their start.

TO DO LIST

- Revise your offer acceptance procedure – ideally with online document signature or physically bringing in signed documents and payroll information

- Build in a process to confirm and log resignation date

- Create a process to book and log a follow up on resignation date

- Create and book a team social event between resignation date and start date

- Schedule two catch up calls

- Create email sequence for pre-onboard

Tools

To download some great templates to help you or for further videos, coaching and resources visit:

www.rec2recsecrets.com/book/downloads

STEP SEVEN: YOUR TALENT ATTRACTION PROCESS – ONBOARDING

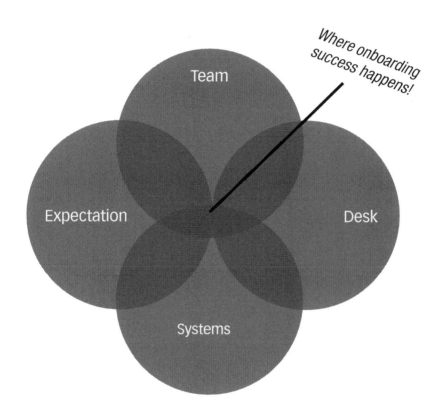

Notes

Remember – your ideal outcome from your new placement is that they integrate with the team well, become productive quickly; and stay. A robust onboarding process makes sure everyone is aware of the expectations set and has an agreed plan of action. Your preparation here is about creating a templated process and agreeing who in your team contributes and when.

TO DO LIST

- Decide who hosts inductions.

- Create induction template document with review dates.

- Create a team induction template (PDF).

- Create a new starter system checklist and nominate contributors.

- Create a desk preparation template and allocate.

- Create date triggers via automated sequence.

- Create a week 1- 4 project plan.

- Nominate Buddies internally for new starters.

Tools

For a set of great FREE templates you can download and edit or more resources to help you implement a winning onboarding process visit

www.rec2recsecrets.com/book/downloads

CONCLUSION

And so my fellow Recruiters, my work here is done…for now.

I hope you have found value in what I have shared with and more importantly can identify with some of the common issues that hurt our businesses.

My hope is that you now feel encouraged enough to take the steps needed to transform your business and allow it to achieve its full potential.

I really do love to hear your stories and updates and I am always happy to answer any questions you may have. Just email me via

tara@rec2recsecrets.com

If you'd like to join a mentoring group, or want to gain more support, tools or books as they are released then please do join my mailing list. I plan for this to be the first of many new tools that I create for my fellow recruitment leaders.

You can sign up here:

www.rec2recsecrets.com/join

Whatever you do next, I wish you every success, but whatever you do, please take one step NOW towards making a change to your business.

I know once you do the rest will follow.

Good Luck
Tara x

ABOUT THE AUTHOR

Tara Lescott is founder of award-winning Rec2Rec agency Recruiter Republic.

Following a 13 year career in recruitment with Hays Plc where she joined as a Trainee and gained promotions rapidly to Manager, Senior Manager, Regional Director and Group Director based on record breaking results (many of which remain today), Tara launched Recruiter Republic to address a severe shortage of talent for the recruitment industry.

Since inception in 2010, Tara has been on a mission to transform the careers of recruiters and recruitment businesses. During this time Tara has developed a team that have worked with over 300 UK recruitment businesses, serving as both Rec2Rec agency and business advisory.

Regular columnist for Recruiter Magazine, Fellow of the IRP, founding member of Women in Recruitment, Judge at Recruiter Awards 2014, 2015, 2016, 2017 and 2018, Judge for Investing in Talent Awards 2015, 2016 and 2017 and regular speaker at events such as Recruitment Expo, Tara is well known for her forthright views on recruitment, her no-nonsense approach to finding answers, her utter fascination with all things digital and technology and a total commitment to raising the profile of the recruitment industry as a whole.

Self-confessed recruitment geek, Tara loves nothing more than talking recruitment to anyone who will listen, whether they like it or not!

Tara lives in Cambridge with her husband Richard and two children.

WANT MORE?

Made in the USA
Columbia, SC
24 April 2018